More Bad Dates

More Bad Dates

And Other Tales from the Dark Side of Love

Carole Markin

BOOKS

RENAISSANCE BOOKS
Los Angeles

Library of Congress Cataloging-in-Publication Data

Markin, Carole.
    More bad dates, and other tales from the
    dark side of love / Carole Markin.
        p. cm
    ISBN 1-58063-016-2 (trade paper : alk. paper)
    1. Dating (Social customs)—Humor.   I. Title
    PN6231.D3M365 1998
    306.73'02'07—dc21   98–14773
                                                              CIP

Design by Tanya Maiboroda

Manufactured in the United States
Distributed by St. Martin's Press

Acknowledgments

I could have not have written this book without the help of many people. They include: Howard Markin, Lois Markin, Robert Markin, Steve Berman, Jeanne Lucas, Evan Cohen, Martin Keleti, Ed Sussman, Jeff Zaslow, Jody Siegler, David Lewis, Danica Kombol, Mark Philips, Sylvia Stein, Benjamin Krepak, James Greenberg, Vikram Jayanti, Joy Scott, Albert Spevak, Mel Markon, Boyce Harman, Nancy Silverman, Nicole Dillenberg, and others I may have forgotten who told me about somebody who knew somebody who had a great story. I am grateful to my agent, Anne McDermott, and her assistants Tiffany Walker and Patrick Bishop. I greatly appreciate the efforts and suggestions of my editor Brenda Scott Royce, the marketing expertise of Michael Dougherty and Kathryn Mills, designers Tanya Maiboroda and Kevin Corcoran, as well as the support of Bill Hartley, Jim Parish, and the other folks at Renaissance Books.

Contents

Introduction

When I decided to write my first book, *Bad Dates: Celebrities (and Other Talented Types) Reveal Their Worst Nights Out,* I had no idea how much it would change my life. I expected to jump through hoops to land the celebrity interviews the book required, but I didn't anticipate my new status as an instant love expert. In retrospect, I shouldn't have been surprised. Our society loves to pigeonhole people. So do TV and radio show bookers who are always hungry for sexy topics and specialists to talk about them. Soon, I became the unofficial Dr. Ruth of Bad Dating.

I also became "Dr. Ruth" to many non-celebrities who decided to confess their own romantic secrets to me. Strangers came up to me at parties. People pulled me aside at family gatherings and funerals. Others snagged me in the green room before TV interviews and during commercial breaks on live radio. Friends called me on their car phones on the way home from their latest dating fiascoes and solicited advice. A few sent referrals. Relatives pawned off lost souls. Even boyfriends got into the act. During one very heated moment during what seemed to be a great date, a new boyfriend suddenly recounted a rather sticky encounter—which he thought was hot and hilarious—then asked me to reciprocate by telling him a story that would titillate him as much as he assumed his tale excited me. The proposition seemed perfectly logical to him. From his perspective, I had to be a sexual savant. I'd heard it all from celebrities and others; I must know what it takes to make a man tick, and I must love an audience for my stories. After that, I considered abandoning the project (and that boyfriend) or sticking out a shingle and charging.

Instead, I've tried to do something better. I've written a second book dedicated to the romantic mishaps of the not-so-famous (like you and me). Some of these true stories were culled from contests that were run in association with the publication of *Bad Dates*. Others came from referrals and chance encounters. A few found their way to me via the Internet. A postal clerk saw the name Bad Dates Inc. on my business checks and volunteered to tell me enough stories to fill a whole volume.

The stories I've selected represent the dark side of love in all of its shadings—the comedic, the terrifying, the bizarre, the sexy, and the tender. And most importantly, the all-too-human. They tell of high hopes and dismal expectations, sexual fantasies and the naked truth. Spanning the decades from World War II to the late 1990s, they include a wide range of complications: from old flames to new allergies, from unruly animals to overly proper in-laws, from religious restrictions to criminal liberties, from clandestine cyber couplings to a not-so-secret ménage à quatres. The storytellers hail from a variety of races and ages, professions and economic strata, as well as both sexes. To my surprise, I found men as anxious to confide as women. Perhaps this reflects the fact that society offers men fewer opportunities to safely tell their tales. Or maybe they've had more bad experiences in their search for perfect partners since they often take the risky first step of asking women out.

The process of collecting the material was never dull. I got to speak with people across the social spectrum, in all parts of America and Canada. As we chatted, I became convinced that sharing these anecdotes could be as helpful to others as it was to me. These tales reassure us that we are not alone in our less-than-perfect romantic lives. Lots of people make mistakes. In fact, some individuals make even more disastrous blunders than our own. So take heart!

Elvis the Pharmacist

JULIA JACOB
*Julia is a teacher certified in
gifted education and special education.
She has two children and lives in
Savannah, Georgia.*

I had just been majorly dumped by my boyfriend in college and I was thoroughly morose. My life was over. My heart was broken. I was going to become a nun. Before I did that, my friends thought I should go out with somebody older, a pharmacist they knew. They said he had many interesting hobbies and always took a girl on a nice date.

When he picked me up, I was surprised that he was so unattractive. He was very heavy and had greasy, thinning hair that was combed back into a pompadour, despite the fact that he couldn't have been more than thirty years old. He wore a shirt with an open collar and a light-colored polyester vest, high-heeled shoes, and chains around his neck. The overall effect was a Vegasy-'70s look. This was 1980.

His car was an older model Cadillac. As soon as we climbed in he said, "This is the car just like the one Elvis used to drive."

I didn't know who he was talking about at first and asked, "Elvis who?"

"The King. The King," he replied with a certain reverence.

Right then it all started to make sense. The chain around his neck was *just like the ones Elvis used to wear*. The platform shoes were *just like the ones Elvis used to don*. The vest, the open shirt, the pompadour, and the half-and-half sunglasses— dark on the top, light on the bottom—were all *just like the ones Elvis used to sport*. And the music... Well, he popped a cassette into the deck and started to sing. Elvis was a beautiful singer. This man was not.

When he ordered dinner, he requested fried peanut butter sandwiches, *just like the ones Elvis used to eat*. I asked him if he would mind if I ordered a salad. He said that would be just fine, because he liked his women thin *just like Elvis did*. This comment led to a discussion of several women who had been important in Elvis's life. He told me what a traitor Priscilla had been. That she'd really turned her back on Elvis when he needed her most. In contrast there was somebody at the end whom he adored. "She was the only one who had been a decent white woman," he said. I didn't know what he meant by that because I couldn't recall Elvis having had any interracial relationships.

He then asked me where I was when I heard Elvis had died. "At the bathhouse in summer camp," I chirped, actually amazed that I remembered at all.

"I was at home, alone, when I got the news," he said very solemnly. Then he mused about whether Elvis was really alive or dead.

I asked him how he knew so much about the King. He claimed to have read everything any studio or record company had ever turned out on him. But his best information came from an inside source—someone who knew someone who knew someone who worked on cars for Vernon Presley. This was pretty much his claim to fame. So much so that he mentioned it several times throughout the night.

The evening became so excruciating, I decided to talk about my biology classes at college. "You know Elvis himself didn't do too well in school," he reminded me. "He didn't have much help at home." I should have known.

Desperate to stay clear of Elvis, I brought up the one topic we hadn't touched—my date's job at the discount drug store. Of course the pharmacist knew all about *the drugs Elvis used to take.* "Those drugs were lethal. He didn't know what he was doing. They were stealing him blind and just feeding him drugs to keep him fat and quiet." Once again he mused if Elvis was alive or dead. This time I didn't even pick up his cue.

My friends were waiting for me when I got back to the dorm. I was distraught. "He was a completely dysfunctional, Elvis-entranced person. I felt so sorry for the guy." After a long, sympathetic silence, my friends burst out laughing. The person who fixed up the date knew all along that the pharmacist had this problem. They figured I would realize right away that the date was a joke and would just go along with it because it was funny. Unfortunately, I was still so upset over my recent heartbreak, I failed to see the humor. Now, of course, I clearly do.

The Ten Commandments

VICTORIA TRAHAN
*Victoria is corporate marketing director
for "Q the Sports Club," a chain of
health and fitness centers. At the time
of her date, she taught courses on
professional goal setting. She lives
in Houston, Texas.*

Dotty, the office manager for one of my consulting clients, had a man she wanted me to meet. "You'll really enjoy dating him," she assured me, "and you won't have anything to worry about."

"Why?" I asked, having been a victim of too many bad dates.

"He's the minister of our church," she said proudly, "which as you know, happens to be one of the biggest churches around. Besides that he's forty-five, has all his hair, and is a very sweet man."

That night I called the minister and he was just delightful. We arranged to meet for lunch the next day. I'm a very punctual person and usually arrive at least five minutes early to any meeting. He showed up ten minutes late, but with this beautiful little card. He explained that he had to go to four different places to find the perfect one because he wanted it to be just right. The card had a tiny bunny on the front and a caption that read, "Just want you to know, I thought of you today." To this he added, "I hope our friendship grows," signed Bob. I thought that was real cute and appreciated the trouble he had gone to on one day's notice.

As soon as the waitress left the table with our order he said, "Vicky, I'm gonna send Dotty to the eye store to get her some glasses, because you're so much more beautiful than what she said, I just can't believe it!" Well, I couldn't believe Dotty told me he had all his hair. All four of them, that is. He was one of those Dairy Queen kind of guys who let it grow out of one side and wind it around and around until the whole top of their head is covered. None of that mattered to me, however, because he was such a charming and witty conversationalist.

He told me he was a widower with a four-teen-year-old daughter and his wife had died ten years before. I told him that in addition to business consulting, I taught courses on professional goal setting. That immediately piqued his interest. "I'm a goal setter," he said. "I set a goal for so many things in my life. For instance, I set a goal for the perfect lady for myself." At that moment I started to feel a little tense, but I thought I'd better just ride this thing out.

"There are ten things that are really important to me in a woman, Vicky," he elaborated. "And what I do is, I write 'em on a piece of paper in descending order and carry 'em in my billfold."

"You do?" I asked, dreading the worst.

"I do," he replied with genuine sincerity. "You see, I meet so many lovely ladies, but if they only have three of the ten things on my list, well then that's only 30 percent, and I can't really be encouraged by a 30 percenter. However, I know that one day, if I continue to look, I'll find what I want."

I told him I agreed with his strategy and watched with amazement as the good minister, the guy who had just entertained me with delightful conversation for half an hour, whipped out two typed, Xeroxed copies of a list entitled "Perfect Woman" and handed me the fresher copy. I thought, how kind of him to make me a copy so that I could qualify myself right here on the spot. Which is, of course, what we proceeded to do, one by one.

Number One on the list: She must be a "Christian." Number Two: "Pretty with a good figure." Number Three: "Big boobs." (You will note, as a separate item from good figure.) I'm a 40 Double D, so I guess I qualified for that one.

Number Four: "Honest and open with feelings." Number Five: "Intelligent and a good conversationalist." Number Six: "Athletic." Number Seven: "Has children and wants more."

When we got to that one, he inquired if my "baby factory was still working." I told him that at thirty-seven I didn't plan to make any babies intentionally. In response, he recited every story ever known to man about childbearing women over forty.

Number Eight followed nicely from Number Seven: "Good cook." She must be able to make nice balanced meals for her family. Number Nine: "Affectionate." And Number Ten: "Loves sex." Thank you, Reverend!

I wanted to laugh, but the psychologist doesn't laugh at the patient. Especially when that patient is a sincere, upstanding man in the community.

The review of the ten items took half an hour, during which time the good minister proposed to me twice. I reminded him that I didn't have children or want more, so I couldn't possibly meet his criteria. He replied, "If eight out of the ten are there, or an 80 percenter, it's workable." Eighty percent? I couldn't quite understand how he came up with that figure, because there was no way for him to really gauge if I loved sex from a thirty-minute discussion.

Needless to say, I didn't accept his two proposals. But that didn't discourage him from asking me if I'd accompany him to Oshman's so he could buy a pair of running shoes.

I looked across the parking lot and saw there was an Oshman's within walking distance. I said "okay," thinking I'd walk across the street, spend two minutes in the store, and then head for my car.

Well, as we strolled outside he invited me to get in his $200 car with a rusty floor. Assuming that he was feeling lazy or chivalrous and wanted to ferry me across the parking lot, I climbed into his dirty jalopy in my $300 skirt. Instead he zoomed out onto the freeway and drove fourteen miles to *another* Oshman's.

At Oshman's he looked, but didn't buy. He invited me to get married once again, but I didn't buy. Then he announced that he planned to spend the rest of the afternoon running my errands with me. I said, "Well, I really need to do some things today that don't include a number two along, so...why don't you just call me sometime?"

He never did. I guess after three out of three rejections, or as he'd put it, "a 100 percenter," the minister gave up. Too bad. The spark just wasn't there.

Love Dis-Connection

SAM KAUFMAN
*After spending years pursuing
asceticism in the temples and
nightclubs of Bangkok, Sam now
finds enlightenment in his 1966 Jaguar,
seventeen Eames chairs and a Chinese
fiancée. He is a trader.*

I am a fervent anti-yuppie, but put a tie around my neck and I make a very convincing replica of the enemy. This attribute was not lost on a certain shady character who spied me walking out of an office building one afternoon several years ago. "You wanna be on *Love Connection*?" he hissed from the shadows. In Los Angeles, one is constantly solicited by people trying to give away tickets to TV shows.

"No thanks," I countered. "I make a lousy audience member. I laugh loudly, but in the wrong places." Then I realized he wasn't offering me mere tickets, he was asking if I wanted to actually appear on *The Love Connection*. I had just been dumped by a girl I'd been seeing for several months and was still licking my wounds. Was I so desperate to meet a girl that I would appear on an idiotic game show? Yes!

Forty minutes later I found myself being interviewed on videotape for the show, and two weeks after that I got a call from a *Love Connection* staff person cheerily congratulating me on having been chosen, based on my videotape, out of a batch of three men. The chooser was a divorced copy machine saleswoman named Tiffany. Our date was to be subsidized by the show's producers to the tune of seventy-five dollars, though the specifics would be left to Tiffany and me.

Tiffany lived in a suburb of Los Angeles that seemed closer to New Mexico than L.A. On the way back to civilization, Tiffany asked with a seriousness reserved for sacred ritual, that I, in the course of our date, treat her like a lady. What the hell did that mean? My last girlfriend was a Marxist lesbian. The word *lady* left her vocabulary when Eisenhower left office. Nevertheless, I assured Tiffany that I would respect her wishes and initiated a polite conversation about copying machines.

By the time we reached the famous Greek restaurant where the waiters whoop it up to Zorba-style Greek music and smash plates on the floor, I was qualified to give advice about copying machines to unsuspecting office managers. I picked this Greek place not out of a love of Mediterranean cuisine, but because I figured it would make good TV. Unfortunately, because of the location of our table, the plates the waiters chose to smash were ours, half-eaten food and all. Each broken plate was immediately replaced by a fresh one, with a brand new portion of steaming Greek food, which Tiffany and I happily ate and ate.

During the dinner, Tiffany revealed a taste for ouzo, which in turn encouraged her to reveal her other tastes, namely, the sports of hunting, fishing, and telling dirty jokes with the guys. Hunting and fishing are hardly more interesting than copying machines to me, so I asked Tiffany to tell me her favorite dirty joke, but she couldn't remember any. I volunteered one of my own, but she didn't laugh. Now this particular joke has never failed me before, so I figured that her hobby of telling jokes derived more from being with the guys on those hunting and fishing trips than from the jokes.

The guys, it turned out, were her husband's buddies, and her husband, from whom she had been divorced *only two weeks*. He was a die-hard career marine, who demanded that Tiffany address him as "sir," as in "yes, sir" and "no, sir." None of this information was being offered to me with any suggestion of abuse or regret. In fact, her divorce resulted from something unrelated to her ex-husband's insistence on sadistic discipline.

I've always enjoyed, even preferred, neurotic women. Yet here I was, faced with a woman who should've been more screwed up than any girl I had ever met and she reeked of normalcy. I didn't know how to react.

Phase two of the date took place at a spa in a luxurious L.A. hotel owned by and catering to the Japanese and specializing in shiatsu massage. Like the Greek restaurant, I figured the massage would make good TV.

Tiffany seemed excited by the prospect of her first shiatsu until she stepped out of her dressing room and was led into a single room with two massage tables, a yard apart. I was already standing there. We were both wearing very skimpy hospital-type gowns, clearly tailored to fit diminutive Japanese businessmen. Tiffany was almost as tall as I (I'm 6'1"), and a lot more voluptuous, so her gown was, shall we say, inadequate. Tiffany instantly assumed the whole massage thing was a devious plot to defile her. Hoping to correct her misconception, I struck up a conversation about copying machines, as two tiny Japanese grannies leapt off the floor and onto our backs.

Personally, I enjoyed having my connective tissue rearranged for forty-five minutes, but as I looked over at Tiffany, I realized her masochism was limited to marrying marines. She was in deep pain. With gallons of Greek food gurgling in her stomach, poor Tiffany was trying hard not to vomit.

The remedy she suggested for her queasiness was rather unusual—a large root beer float.

Unsure of the medical wisdom, I nevertheless took Tiffany to a nice little Denny's I happen to know. In Denny's, Tiffany was very much at home.

Phase three of the date took place at a Hollywood nightclub dedicated to "sixties favorites." Unfortunately, Tiffany was immediately put off by the crowd, whom she described as "hardcore punk rockers." To me, they looked like ordinary college kids having rather wholesome fun.

In spite of her prejudices, Tiffany managed to have a good time dancing, and so did I. The long drive back to her house was pleasant, and when we pulled up, Tiffany somewhat nervously invited me in. In my circles, being invited inside a woman's home at the end of an evening out is not necessarily a license to transform oneself into Bob Guccione. Yet, why would a woman who asked to be treated *like a lady* tempt fate by making herself vulnerable? Was this to be a test of my machismo?

Up until this point on the date, I had hardly thought about the whole TV thing. Now, I felt the hot breath of thirty million Americans leaning over my shoulder, waiting for my next move.

When Tiffany flipped on the light in her living room, I half-expected to see a dozen marines arm wrestling each other on the carpet, but instead, all I could see were stuffed animals, everywhere. Her ex-husband had obviously cleaned up at a lot of carnivals and country fairs.

She took me on a quick tour of her pad, which, apart from the stuffed animals and a picture of Jerry Falwell, was essentially a shrine to the United States Marines.

Tiffany asked me if I wanted a drink. Affecting a "Bond, James Bond" indifference and brushing a plush hippo off the couch, I coolly asked for a bourbon and water. She didn't have bourbon. She didn't have scotch. She didn't have beer. But she did have water.

So water we both had, mine drunk on the couch, hers on a chair facing me. She became very apprehensive here. Having no idea why, I decided to give up.

I got up, thanked Tiffany for a wonderful time, and was about to kiss her goodnight when she looked at me with a bewildered expression worthy of Dan Quayle. Either she completely hated my guts or she was deeply insulted that I hadn't tried anything. Terrified of violating her sense of ladiness, I quickly surveyed my options. I ended up shaking her hand.

Tiffany and I were interviewed for the show separately by telephone, and two weeks later we showed up at the studio for the show's taping. After being made-up, I waited in the green room with the other male contestants. They all got along swimmingly with each other, down to swapping phone numbers of their TV dates.

I was pretty nervous when my turn came up, additionally so because of the script the producers had given me to memorize earlier in the day. It only contained lines culled from my post-date interview. What Tiffany would say remained a mystery to me.

During the taping, Tiffany and I were kept apart. First they showed clips of the three guys she chose from, including me. Why she chose me, I'll never know, because the other two would've been perfect for her—outdoorsy types who probably enjoy hunting prairie dogs with flame-throwers. Then Chuck Woolery, that monument to TV smoothness, asked Tiffany to describe the date. Her version portrayed me as a hardcore punk rock pervert. Evidently my custom-made Italian cashmere sports jacket and Brooks Brothers pants were not conservative enough for her, because as she told it, as soon as she opened her door and saw me, she knew it wouldn't work out—I was far too "Hollywood," while she considered herself "Beverly Hills." It was obvious to me that I could not follow the little script they gave me, because the way things were proceeding, I was going to take the rap for a bad date.

My improvisations during the taping, while prompting much laughter from the studio audience and the stage crew, did not meet with approval from the producers, who brilliantly re-cut the videotape to reduce me to Jerry Lewis minus the humor. Every good comeback I made was chopped right out, and even my grandmother, to whom I am the living incarnation of Moses, Buddha, and Abraham Lincoln combined, was ashamed of me. The last thing Chuck Woolery said to me on the show was, "Sam, not a great date, huh?" My response, which like the others was edited out, was "Chuck, I'm happy as long as I get the microwave."

Rubber Necking

JOYCE CUSTER
*Joyce worked in the billing department
of a locomotive company. She now
lives in Florida.*

It was a Saturday night and I had butterflies in my stomach as I rushed to slip into my Playtex girdle. Needing something to hold on to, I ran my fingers through one of the air holes and tore the soft rubber a wee bit as I pulled it up. I thought, well, I'll just put a piece of tape on it and it'll be all right. It was the only girdle I owned and I had to wear it under my nice, navy crepe dress. I had bought the dress especially for my third date with the high school football star, a man one year my junior, which was quite unusual in 1949. That dress was so lovely. It had a tulip skirt that tapered around the calf and forced a girl to walk with little tiny steps.

At that time, nobody had cars. So we hopped on the bus and rode uptown to the Ohio Theater, one of the vintage movie palaces in Lima, Ohio. It was *the* place to take a date and the balcony was *the* place to sit.

Oh, that theater was gorgeous! There were circular staircases on both sides of the lobby. Between the staircases there were big, crystal chandeliers that hung down low enough for you to walk past the glistening pieces as you climbed.

Here I was taking tiny steps in my tulip skirt as we ascended the fifty magical steps to the exquisite balcony when...*plop*! I grabbed the rail as I tripped and lunged forward. Totally confused, I looked down to see if I'd somehow stepped on my skirt. Instead I found my Playtex girdle split in half around my ankles. Still in one piece, it was hanging on to my suspenders like some desperate hooked fish. I reached down and tried to undo the garters, but between my tight skirt and my nerves, I just couldn't do it. Traffic jammed up on the crowded stairs. People stared. I was mortified.

My date felt so sorry for me and tried to shield me as much as he could. "This could happen to anybody," he said, "Enjoy it!" Enjoy it? The sweeter he was to me, the worse I felt.

My mood didn't phase him. He simply picked up the split girdle and slid it inside his coat. "Come on now. The restrooms are right up here at the top of the steps." Later we had quite a laugh wondering what people would think when they discovered a girdle in the wastepaper basket of the men's room.

Meanwhile, in the ladies' room, I took my hose off and threw them away. When I came back out, I couldn't face my date. Somehow I forced myself to sit there, bare legged, and watch *The Third Man* with Joseph Cotten.

To this day, I cannot forget that night or that movie. When it played on TV not very long ago, I still couldn't watch it.

Unclear and Present Danger

KERRY LEVIN
Kerry is an architect and developer working in the Chicago area.

I got on online and I met this girl from Chicago named Laurie who seemed like the perfect quality life partner for me. At thirty-four, she was so successful as a personal injury attorney, she had decided to retire and write a novel. She said she owned a spacious, older home in a nice suburb outside Chicago and was attractive—5'4", 110 pounds, with long brown hair. Besides that she was witty, worldly, well traveled, and had never been married. Quite an unusual package compared to what I normally meet here in Chicago. The one hitch was that she was in the process of healing from a broken engagement to a fairly prominent person. I asked her who the person was. She was evasive. But after baiting me for several days, I guessed the name: Tom Clancy, the bestselling author. She'd met him through an online writers' forum and somehow wound up dating him.

Laurie had all these really interesting stories about traveling around the country to meet Clancy in secret because he was still married at the time. They'd take separate planes, and Clancy's bodyguard—who was always hitting on her—would pick Laurie up at the airport and take her via some unusual route to a prearranged spot, thereby avoiding the press. From all these stories and various other innuendo, I deduced that Laurie was really good looking. Not surprisingly, after he officially announced his divorce, Clancy asked her to get married.

I was hot to meet Laurie right away. Unfortunately she was leaving for a trip to Costa Rica with her sister. When she got back, we tried to hook up, but never did. Finally we lost touch. About six months later, she resurfaced online. I figured she'd had enough time to mourn Tom and was now ready for a new relationship.

We talked on Monday while we were both at the office and planned to meet that Friday night. I was so excited, I got ants in my pants. I had to meet Laurie that day.

So, as soon as I hung up the phone, I typed a subpoena—subpoenaing her to dinner. Then I bought a single rose and traced her phone number back to her office address. It was in the Schaumburg area, which has some beautiful, all-glass, office buildings. I assumed that given her status as a retiring attorney, her suite would be in one of those high-rises.

I got in my car and went out searching. Her office, it turned out, was in the middle of some back alley industrial park. The building itself was a single-story, brown brick, industrial, incubator structure with slot windows and a small warehouse at the back. Her suite had no sign on the door and no number. In fact, you had to deduce the number by looking at the numbers of the adjacent suites. Not as monumental as I thought, to say the least.

I creaked open the door. There was no furniture in the reception area. I looked around and thought, "this is weird." I said hello. There was no answer. "Maybe she's more retired than I realized," I said to myself, still trying to give her the benefit of the doubt.

I opened the next door and creaked my way further in. There was still nobody around. Then I saw one office with the door partly ajar and heard papers rustling. I walked over, pushed open the door and found this little gnome-like person sitting on a Samsonite folding chair hunched over a file cabinet. "Excuse me," I said politely, "Is Laurie here?"

The woman looked up and snapped at me in a harsh, crotchety voice, "I'm Laurie. Who are you?" She must have weighed about 150 pounds. She was short, dumpy, and nasty to boot.

"I'm Kerry," I replied through a cheerful smile that masked my disappointment.

"What the hell are you doing here?" she asked angrily.

"Making a mistake, apparently," I said as I turned around, with my rose and my subpoena, and walked out.

I was trembling as I got back in my car. On the drive home, I began replaying every conversation we'd ever had in my mind. I just couldn't believe it. How could my judgment have been so far off? Here I thought I was meeting a Mary Ann from *Gilligan's Island*-type with all the trappings of a successful lawyer, a nice office with high quality art and a bustling staff, and instead I encountered some mean nickel-and-dime attorney who was fat and dowdy. She could never have dated Tom Clancy! She probably sent him e-mail and *thought* she was dating him.

Then again, her descriptions of flying around the country and meeting him and being picked up by his bodyguard and taking circuitous routes to avoid the press were all very believable. But if you've ever been conned by a con artist, you know that they have a talent for getting into minutia that completely takes your mind off the fact that you're being conned.

I went back to my office and tried to compose myself and get back into my work. It was very difficult. I was so disturbed and distraught.

About a week later, she was back online innocently asking if I wanted to hook up soon. I never responded.

That experience taught me a lesson. If you correspond with someone too long online without meeting them in person, they're hiding something. And try not to meet anyone without a photo.

Off to the Wrong Foot

KAREN FULKS
*Having sampled jobs from
forklift operator to church secretary,
Karen now runs a business organizing
other people's lives. She recently found
the perfect husband as the result
of a blind date.*

The most common call I received when I worked at the L.A. Sex Help Line was "I'm lonely. Where can I meet people?" I had my rap: take a class, go to your temple or your church, ask your friends, or answer personal ads. After my divorce, I had taken classes and met people who were only eighteen years old, gone to a couple of temple dances that were worse than high school proms, and slept with all of my friends. So personal ads seemed like the only option left.

Part of the reason I answered the one I found in the Jewish paper was the guy's interest in meeting an "ex-hippie." I figured that meant he smoked dope, which, at the time, was cool with me.

"Are you ready?" he asked as I opened my front door and met a guy who was neither a scumbag nor a heartthrob. He was just your average, dark-haired Yugoslavian who said he was into spiritual things.

"Yeah, I'm ready," I replied. "Are you?"

He paused for a moment before responding thoughtfully, "Let's see, uh, I've got my shoe horn, and I've got my hand lotion, and I've got something else . . ."

"What?" I asked, not knowing what could possibly come after those two objects in any sequence on an IQ test.

"I can't put my finger on it, but I'm ready."

We got into my car. I turned on the heat and started to drive down the street. Out of the corner of my eye, I saw him fiddling with something, but I couldn't figure out what it was. Finally, curiosity got the better of me and I turned my head. He'd pulled a black ski mask completely over his face!

I was so shocked the only thing I could think was, "Don't tell me this is the third item on the IQ test!" Of course I didn't say that. I gulped and asked what he was doing.

"I found out today that you lose 80 percent of your body heat out of the top of your head," he replied with complete earnestness. "I couldn't find a hat and this is all I had. You don't mind, do you? I promise I'll take it off in the theater."

You know how sometimes you want a relationship so badly you will overlook anything? That's where my head was at at that time because otherwise I would have gone straight to the police.

Instead, I continued driving to the theater with this man in a ski mask. And sure enough, just before we walked in the door, he removed it.

As soon as we found our seats at the end of a row of thirty-three interconnected chairs, he said, "You don't mind if I meditate, do you?"

"Excuse me?"

"I'm a little off-center..." That's for sure. I guess that was what he meant by spiritual things, huh?

Next, he took his metal shoe horn out of his back pocket, pried off his penny loafers, and dropped them into the middle of the narrow aisle. He then grabbed the sides of his feet, lifted them up quickly, and crossed them underneath himself in a semi-lotus position. This movement sent a shock wave down the row of connected chairs. Everybody turned their heads to see my date, who by now had his hands facing upwards, his eyes closed, and his lips emitting a low "mnnnnn." When the house lights dimmed, he popped out of his trance.

The play was called *Decadence*, and as you can imagine from the title, it was filled with every cuss word in the English language. That's no big deal to me, but when the lead actor said the first four letter word, my date bellowed with laughter. Every time one of these words came up, which was like every other word, his laughter got louder and more physical until finally the whole row of people wanted to kill him.

At intermission he gleefully announced that this was the funniest play he had ever seen. I said, "Well, it's obvious that you found it very, very amusing. By the way, what was the last play that you saw?"

"*The Music Man.*"

"*The Music Man?*" I thought, rolling my eyes. "No wonder he's laughing."

As we walked out to my car after an even more humiliating second act, I said to myself, "Karen, you always try to look for the good in people, but at this point you must realize that you do not want to be seen in public with this guy. What are you going to do?"

"Let's go back to my house and I'll make some tortellini," I offered. He thought that sounded like a great idea.

The instant we got back to my apartment he pried off his penny loafers and started examining my books. Soon the tortellini was finished. I scooped it onto two plates, set them both out on the kitchen counter, then turned back to the stove and started to make the cream sauce. From behind me I heard him say, "Do you mind if I sit on your counter?"

"There isn't much room," I replied, "but you can sit on the edge or something." He hopped up with a thud and immediately asked if I wanted some hand lotion.

Pissed, I turned around to him to say, "I'm making cream sauce, what would I do with hand lotion?" but the words caught in my throat when I saw him sitting there in semi-lotus position with his stocking feet in a dish of tortellini. "Excuse me, forget the hand lotion, would you get your feet out of my tortellini?"

"This isn't your tortellini," he pouted. "This is mine."

I grabbed the pasta, "I don't care whose tortellini this is. Get your feet out of the tortellini!"

He looked at me like I was a crazy woman. "I don't know why you're so bent out of shape," he complained.

"Maybe it's just a funny thing with me, but when people put their smelly, grimy feet in my tortellini it just sort of grosses me out. So go!"

He soon left with an empty stomach.

Disco Discombobulation

ARTHUR BARRY MILLER

*Arthur runs a disc jockey service that
provides music for weddings, parties,
and nightclubs in Arizona.*

My job was new. My car was new. My underwear was new. My friends, furniture, and apartment were new. I was ripe for a new relationship. The married coed I desired had a Christie Brinkley-type cousin who was newly single. Could she be the girl for me?

Despite my distaste for blind dates I got the number, made the call, set the date, took a shower, flossed. With a minimum of fuss I found her apartment in a giant, beehive-like complex in a nice suburb of Baltimore. I knocked twice. No answer. Only disco. I knocked harder. Still only disco. I waited about five minutes for a break between songs and knocked again.

She invited me in and locked the door behind us. Not quite ready yet, but still very attractive. She returned to her loft bedroom, door shut, Thelma Houston's larynx working overtime.

There was a knock at the door. "Want me to get that?" I shouted. No answer, only disco.

Through the peephole I saw a big trucker type in a Levi's jacket. Roommate? Brother? Jealous ex-lover? I opened the door, leaving the chain lock still attached (one can never be too careful).

The guy inquired, "Is that your gold Camaro parked outside, buddy?" I could feel bile rising in my throat. "Listen. I don't know how to tell you this," he said, "so I'll just tell you. My old lady accidentally ran into it. Don't worry, she's insured and everything." Don't worry! My beautiful car was three weeks old and had been vacuumed each of those twenty-one days. It had sipped only two tanks of hi-test. We were gonna grow old together.

Just as I removed the chain from the door to survey the damage and meet the metal-mangler, the door burst open and I sailed backwards into the room. From carpet-level I saw three vicious rednecks charge in, one headed straight for me.

I was relieved of my wallet, watch, and beloved high school ring without much of a fight. They caught me off guard. No amount of talk seemed to dissuade them.

My mystery date, meanwhile, was oblivious to the invasion unfolding in her living room. Strains of KC and the Sunshine Band were boogying out from under the bedroom door. When she emerged (looking radiant, I might add), she was treated to the same devaluation, except that she also lost the contents of her jewelry box, everything dumped into an empty pillowcase. We were left gagged and tied to kitchen chairs placed at opposite ends of the apartment as Thelma Houston proclaimed, "Don't Leave Me This Way."

I couldn't see her face, couldn't communicate above the music, and couldn't loosen my bonds. I could, however, study the staircase to her bedroom and the percussive arrangements of the K-Tel disco compilation that droned on...and on.

I still remember the songs in their original order. No wonder—we listened to that endless eight-track tape for nearly five hours before the neighbors called the cops. Ironically, we were violating an after-eleven P.M. noise curfew.

The Apes of Wrath

JEAN MOSTELLER

*Jean is a mother of two who also
has a flex-time sales job in the
pharmaceutical industry. She lives
in San Bernardino, California.*

Marty was a take-charge kind of person and everybody just let him do his thing. He had moved to quiet San Bernardino from aggressive New Jersey during his senior year in high school and had done well for himself because he was blessed with an aptitude for football and remarkable good looks. He was a clean cut, well-built guy with high cheekbones, blue eyes, and blonde hair that swooped across his forehead like a surfer. His only flaw was his big nose. But I could put that aside, because he was so gorgeous.

Dating Marty was like dating a foreigner. I'd never met anyone like him before and was really impressed that he was so worldly, drove a blue Volkswagen bug (in 1966), and was interested in dating a mere sophomore.

In order to impress him back, I spent extra time getting myself ready and selected the perfect outfit for me: burgundy stirrup stretch pants (I thought they were so cool), and a long, multi-colored, angora sweater. The moment Marty saw me he said, "That sweater looks like shit." Right in front of my mother! My mother said nothing. She believed that at fifteen I should make my own decisions about men. So I returned to my bedroom and changed into a long, white, silky over-blouse that was very popular in the sixties. I figured he couldn't say anything bad about plain white.

The plan was for us to pick up another couple, both seniors, in his Volkswagen bug and drive an hour and a half south to the Los Angeles Zoo. To sheltered me, it was very daring to be going on a first date in a car to another city. I also felt pressure because I didn't know the other people from Adam and felt so young.

"Children twelve and under enter for free," Marty read aloud off the sign above the ticket window before slapping down the dollar and fifty cents for a *single* adult admission. "She's twelve," he told the ticket salesman without hesitation. Talk about being mortified! At fifteen, I wore a size 36C bra. Too inexperienced and introverted to say anything, I let it slide. As did the management.

By 11:00 A.M. the zoo was packed. We made our way to the primate cages. Years ago, the zookeepers weren't very strict about what people fed the animals. People tossed popcorn and candy into the cages. The orangutans ate it. Several jokesters threw in cigarette butts and laughed. The other spectators joined in the fun. To me, the whole scene was appalling.

Then one orangutan picked up a cigarette butt that still happened to be lit and burned his fingers. Furious, he scooped up all the things that had landed within his reach and hurled them wildly back at the crowd. The crowd retaliated in jest, lobbing in more junk. In response the orangutan picked up a big pile of fresh manure and heaved it. Bull's-eye! The dung hit me squarely on the left breast of my white silk blouse and splattered all over me.

I looked down at my shirt and surveyed the damage. When you're large-breasted at fifteen, you're already self-conscious about your chest. But when I lifted my eyes from the stain and saw at least fifty people with their eyes glued to me guffawing, I just wanted to die. Marty, too, was drunk with laughter. When he finally sobered up, he said coldly, "Well, do something about that!" I glared at him, thinking, "What am I supposed to do? Take off my shirt right here?"

The other girl in our party felt sorry for me. She steered me to the bathroom where we found some paper towels and spent quite a long time trying to wipe off the manure. Of course, it left a big brown smelly stain. To cover the odor, she poured most of a bottle of cheap Tigress perfume over the blouse. Some combination! I was so humiliated, I could not speak.

When we emerged from the bathroom, Marty was once again Mr. Sensitivity. "Well, couldn't you get the rest of it off?" he complained. Despite his embarrassment, Marty was too tightfisted to call the whole day off and proceeded to drag me around the zoo for the next five hours.

Completely dazed, I trudged along in silent, self-conscious misery without shedding a tear. It was too great a risk. Back then we all wore heavy "Cher" eyeliner on both sides of our eyes. It would have been ten times worse if tears caused the black paint to run down my face.

The hour and a half ride back to San Bernardino was bumpy and loud. It gave me the worst headache. As soon as we pulled up to my house, I jumped out of the car and slammed the door. I didn't even say goodbye.

In retrospect I sometimes wonder if Marty was negatively clairvoyant. After all, he told me my first outfit looked like shit, and the second one literally did.

The Baptist's Daughter

ROYCE JACKSON
*Royce is a psychiatrist practicing
in Tallahassee, Florida.*

Sally was a fun girl in a small country high school in southwest Georgia. All the boys liked her, and she liked all the boys. Although Sally was always extremely friendly to me, I was too shy to do anything about her overtures until the spring of my senior year when I finally got up the nerve to ask her out. "How 'bout Wednesday night," she suggested, "Come to my house at 6:30 and meet my parents."

My friends guaranteed it would be a date that I'd never forget. I figured they were right, since it was going to be my first time making it with a fast girl.

Wednesday night I called for Sally. A Mormon Elder look-alike with a pinstriped suit and tie, a beard and long hair answered the door and introduced himself to me as her father. This stern, primitive Baptist invited me into the living room and brought down his friendly daughter, who was wearing a full skirt, saddle Oxford shoes, and a low-cut top that revealed large breasts. After a polite greeting, Sally's father asked us both to kneel down on the oak floor for a parting prayer before the date.

I followed his lead and prayed for Sally's chastity and safe return, knowing that I was going to have a good time as soon as we walked out the door.

No such luck. "Sally has to go to a prayer meeting over at the church," her father informed me. "That's where you two can go." Then he added, "And you can take along her older sister." Sally's sister was a prim and proper English teacher who played the piano. I was starting to understand why my friends said this date would be one I'd never forget.

At the prayer meeting, the preacher was longer-winded than usual. He even opened the church doors to invite people to join up. One couple accepted, and of course he had to baptize them right there on the spot. I wondered if the straight-laced sister had conspired with him to throw off my plans, because the service ran so far over schedule, I had to take Sally directly home without enjoying one second of the thirty minutes of pleasure I had anticipated.

When we got back to the house, her father was peering out the window waiting for us. To my surprise, he invited me back inside and asked once again if Sally and I would join him on our knees on the oaken floor. This time his prayer seemed like an eternity as he thanked God for Sally's "preserved" chastity and safe return.

The next day in school, I learned what I had done wrong. "You should have taken her out during the day," my friends scoffed. "That way you could have avoided the father." They were right of course. Because despite the prayers for her chastity, Sally was still the most popular girl in school.

A Guy to Die For

GLORIA GAGNE
*Gloria is a published poet, a farmer, and
a professional wedding cake decorator.
She also handles paperwork for her
husband's tractor trailer business.
She lives in Maine.*

One of my best friends, Joy, said she had a cousin coming into town whom "I would die for." She claimed he was tall and muscular with sandy blonde hair and blue eyes, and he really wanted to date me. I told her I really wanted to meet him, but I didn't know if I'd be able to arrange it. My very strict parents wouldn't allow me to date at fifteen. "Let me talk to my parents," I said.

I gave it my best shot and my parents agreed. "As long as he's Joy's relative," they conceded, "But he's got to come here first so we can meet him." That was fine because he was supposed to pick me up at 6:00 for a double date with Joy and her boyfriend.

Six o'clock came and my father yelled up the stairs. Actually, yelled is an understatement. He called me down and demanded, "Who is this man?!"

To my surprise, there was this very nice looking thirty-eight-year-old *adult* standing at the front door. "Someone must be playing a joke on me," I said. "I don't know him."

"He says he's your date for the night," my father replied. Then he cast me one of those looks that could kill. I knew I was dead meat.

"My date?" I squeaked. "That can't be Joy's cousin."

"Yes, I am your date," the man informed me. "Joy told me all about you and I've been dying to go out with you."

"Oh, my god—" I gulped.

My father jumped to my defense. "You're not taking my daughter anywhere," he said firmly.

"She's my date and I'm taking her out because I told her I'd take her out and I'm not leaving here until I take her out!" I hovered near the door with my mouth hanging open, praying that my father wouldn't let this gruff man take me anywhere.

"You're *my* age. Are you out of your mind?" my father roared. "I suggest you leave now."

In response, the man pulled a handgun out of his pants pocket and pointed it at my father. "I said I'm not going nowhere until I take your daughter out. Joy fixed us up. I'm taking her out!"

"I don't care who fixed you up. You're not taking her anywhere and you'd better put that thing away." My father slammed the door in his face and locked it.

Instead of leaving, the guy sat down on our front lawn, with his knees up to his chest, and the gun aimed at our front door.

My father was shocked and furious. "What do you intend to do about this, Gloria? How do you expect me to get rid this psycho?" I was too terrified of my father to offer a suggestion. "I ought to kill you," he raged. "First date! Now I know what kind of trouble we're going to have with you."

He didn't have to tell me I was grounded (although he did). I marched back up the stairs and locked myself into my bedroom. I was scared stiff.

For the next five hours, I spied on my armed date from my bedroom window, wringing my hands and praying he wouldn't shoot anybody in my family. Inside, everyone was on pins and needles. The neighbors all around us were calling because they were frightened too. My father was a rock through all of this. He just let the guy sit there out on the lawn, figuring he'd eventually give up and go away.

The man didn't move an inch for those five hours. Finally, my father got sick of the whole thing and called the police. They came, took the gun, took my date, put him in their cruiser and whisked him away.

When I saw Joy at school the next day, I wanted to kill her. "Listen Joy," I demanded, "I want to know what's going on, and *now*! Is he your cousin?"

"He is and he isn't."

"What does that mean?"

"Well...He's been a friend of the family for years and years so we just assume he's my cousin. But we haven't seen him in a while because he's been in prison in New Hampshire until three days ago."

"You didn't tell me this!" I screamed. "What was he in for?"

"Armed robbery and rape," she replied matter-of-factly.

"You must really hate me to do this to me!"

"Well no," she said nonchalantly. "He did his time. He's a nice guy." *Nice guy?* She acted like dating an armed, convicted rapist was a natural thing and I was crazy for being upset.

Every night after that I was petrified. I was certain this man was going to reappear at my door to finish the job. About a week later Joy told me her "cousin" had left town. Still the idea of rape haunted me for months, as did fantasies of what could have happened to my family. I was in such shock, I didn't trust myself or anybody else. I thought, "What if I pick the wrong date next time and my father can't save me?"

Now when I look back at this harrowing incident I find it ironic that Joy told me my blind date would be someone I would die for and I literally almost did.

Stupid Pet Tricks

DAVID MCGEEHAN
*David lives in Pennsylvania where he
works as a computer technician for
IBM. Now married, he loves the arts,
nature, and woodworking.*

On my rounds as a computer technician I met this attractive office manager who asked me out on a date. She lived with her mother and father in the southern part of the Poconos where many Pennsylvania Dutch reside. These people tend to be on the quiet side and keep to themselves. Not being from the area, I tried to approach the situation with an openness that I hoped would get me accepted.

First I met my date's dog Dusty, a Lab mix who was fifty pounds overweight. He trotted up to me. I love dogs, so I petted him 'hi.' Then her mother came downstairs and didn't acknowledge me at all. She just glided past me with her arms full of photo albums, like a walking dream. My date acted like this was normal and told me to follow her mother into the dining room of their dark, old fashioned house.

We sat down, and without any of the standard parental questions, mom opened up the photo albums and started to show me pictures of hot air balloons. She never seemed to have gone up in them. She just visited places where they were launched and took snap shots. As a result, most of the pictures were dots in the sky. Four big albums full of them! I tried to act interested, but there are only so many witty comments you can make about floating rubber.

Later her daughter told me that hot air balloons were her mother's "thing." "In contrast, I'm into butterflies," she explained, noting the oversized, sequined insect on the front of her polyester sweater. It matched her butterfly earrings.

"What's your father into?" I joked.

"Lead," she said matter-of-factly.

"Lead?!"

"He works with lead so he stays upstairs. They think that's what makes him depressed."

"Oh . . ."

It was like a scene out of the movie *Eraserhead*, but without the chicken. Mom's things are lighter than air, dad's into lead, and she's the product of both. This whole family was off-center!

I had planned to take her out to eat and to a nine o'clock movie, but because of the balloon photo show, we were hopelessly late. We raced to the Chinese restaurant I had chosen. It was packed. If we waited we'd miss the movie, so we dashed back out to my car and headed for a new restaurant that I'd heard was nice. It turned out to be a glorified fast-food joint with plasticware and ugly meals.

By the time we made it to the movie the line was long. It was January and about eight degrees outside. We stood there shivering. When we finally reached the window they'd just sold out. I capitulated, "The night's a total disaster. We may as well just go back to your place and watch TV."

We returned to her house and as soon as I walked in the door, her dog, Dusty, the one she picked up as a stray fourteen years before, bounded up to me. I reached down to pet him, and the exact instant my finger touched his head, he fell over and died. I swear to God! When he hit the ground, his bladder emptied, just like I'd heard people do when they're hanged. My date shrieked and burst into tears. I knew I didn't kill this dog by touching his head, but I certainly was the last one to touch him alive. I felt terrible.

I tried to calm her down, but since I hardly knew her, I didn't know the right things to say. I finally managed to get her to just whimper instead of scream, when out of nowhere, Dusty let out this "Hhhh." It was an involuntary action that sounded like he sucked in a big breath of air.

She went crazy again. I appealed to logic, "He's not moving and he emptied himself, that's a sure sign he's dead."

"How do you know?" she cried angrily, "You're not a vet!"

At ten o'clock on a Saturday night she called her vet at home. He agreed to meet us at his office to save a dog that was already dead! At this point, I would have done anything to get out of that house so I decided to go along with her fantasy and pretend Dusty was alive.

The obese dog was starting to get stiff. We tried picking him up by the legs, but, no pun intended, he was just dead weight. Somehow we maneuvered the stinking animal onto the backseat of her car. Despite her crazed state, she insisted on driving.

She drove like a bat out of hell, using red lights as yields, through the back alleys of Allentown until suddenly she had to slam on the brakes. As soon as she did, Dusty rolled off the back seat, turned upside down, and became wedged on the floor between the front and back seats. "Hhhhmmm!" The remaining air in his lungs came out of his throat with a loud grunt.

"You're alive!" my date yelled, as she stepped on the accelerator. She glanced over her shoulder while taking a turn on an unlit road at seventy miles per hour. The sight of Dusty upside down with his legs in the air upset her even more. We practically flew to the vet.

As soon as the poor vet saw Dusty laid out on his table he pronounced him dead. "He's been dead since your date touched his head," he said.

She burst into tears again. It was sad. She did have this dog fourteen years.

I drove her home and told her I'd call during the week to see how she was doing.

On Wednesday, I asked her out again. Although I had known fifteen minutes into our first date that the relationship was doomed, I was guilt-ridden.

The next weekend I found myself in the same dining room seated at the same table. This time mom and dad stayed upstairs, which was a relief. I braced myself for something bizarre, like a showing of her personal collection of butterfly memorabilia, but she threw me off completely by handing me a Styrofoam box that looked like an oblong Big Mac container. Embossed in the top was a dove with an olive branch in its mouth. I opened it cautiously. Inside was a plastic bag filled with charred bones and dust. "It's Dusty," she said in a detached tone. "I had him cremated."

I couldn't believe it. She gave me her dog, the same stinking dog I carted around the week before! "Don't tell me you want me to take this home as a souvenir?" I asked, dreading the worst.

"No," she replied, "I'm burying him at sunrise tomorrow behind his favorite tree in the backyard."

Two seconds later we were out the door and on our way to listen to some live music. She hated the music and hacked and sneezed her way through the set because she had a cold. As soon as it was over, I decided to cut my losses. I took her home, said goodnight, and never asked her out again. Needless to say, I also passed on Dusty's interment.

All Tied Up
and Nowhere to Go

DANIEL FREEMAN
Dan is an artist, a college professor,
and a great surfer.

For a long time, Chloe and I had been trying to get another couple into bed with us, but we couldn't quite figure out how to make it happen. We knew that whatever we did couldn't be obvious, and that we'd need some kind of stimulant like drugs or alcohol to loosen up people's belts.

One night Chloe and I went to a party with my upstairs neighbor Tim and his girlfriend Heather. Tim was a musician who I knew was very sexual. Heather was exactly what you'd expect from a person with her name. She was a blonde, potentially delicious "girl-next-door" type. Chloe, in contrast, was a masseuse by profession and very erotic. I knew she'd had lesbian experiences as well as encounters where more than one couple was having sex in the room at the same time.

So, Tim, Heather, Chloe, and I went to the party, got high, and left together. Tim and Heather returned to Tim's apartment. Chloe and I went back to mine. We slipped into my bedroom and started messing around and talking about a porno movie we'd seen a couple weeks before in which these people were tied up. This inspired Chloe to try that on me.

I took off my clothes and lay down on my back, spread-eagle, on my blue sheets. Using a blue satin cord from my bathrobe, Chloe fastened my arms and legs to the four posts of my big, brass bed. She lit some candles and turned on a warm, seductive light. The atmosphere was great. There was just enough light to see what was happening. Then Chloe took off her clothes and began to work on me. I was getting really excited, when suddenly Chloe disappeared into the living room for a few moments and called Tim. I didn't know what she was up to. I couldn't hear anything and my mind was totally tripped out on fantastic fantasies.

Tim told Heather that Chloe and I had invited them over for a nightcap. Meanwhile, Chloe returned to my bedroom, said nothing, and started going down on me.

Suddenly, the bedroom door flew open and Tim walked in. I thought, "This is possibly quite interesting. Chloe actually pulled off our fantasy." Then Heather burst through the door and the whole mood changed. She was absolutely horrified. Her face was so contorted, it looked like she'd just witnessed someone being run over by a truck. But instead of fleeing the scene of the crime, so to speak, she backed straight up into the farthest recesses of my open closet while continuing to stare at me with this gleeful semi-smile and these big, bulging eyes. Of course, her gaze did wonders for my erection, which took a major nose dive.

The room was absolutely silent. I tried to fill the dead air, but trying to explain your way out of a situation like that is like trying to do a dance with your arms and legs in a full-body straightjacket.

Chloe was equally tongue-tied. She stood up, shifted around the room and babbled something. Her words had no effect: Tim was just as fixated on her naked body as Heather was on mine.

Finally, I stuttered, "Well, um...Maybe you should untie me?" With that, Heather snapped out of shock and beelined out of the room. Tim chased after her. Chloe followed on his heels, leaving me all tied up with nowhere to go.

At that moment, I concluded it's better to fantasize about a having a foursome than to ever again try it.

Get Me to the Morgue on Time

LAURA DAEHLER

A former cancer ward nurse, Laura is now a sales representative for a surgical equipment company. She's newly married and lives in Chicago. Her sister, Martha Staky, a stay-at-home mom with two kids, contributed to this story.

After two and one-half hours of witty conversation over drinks, Tom asked if I'd like to go out some time. As I accepted, I could hear my mother's warning, "Don't accept a date from a guy you just met in a bar. You just don't know anything about him." So I said to him, "By the way, what kind of cars do you fix at your body shop?"

Tom coughed. "Laura, it's not that kind of body shop."

"Well, what other kind is there?"

I couldn't believe I had a date with a mortician! On the other hand, how could I reject him now? We'd had fun talking, and I'd certainly handled my own share of bodies as a cancer ward nurse.

All week long people at the hospital teased me. He'll wear a black suit. He'll show up in a hearse. When he arrived wearing jeans and driving a full-sized station wagon, I chuckled with relief.

We drove forty-five minutes from my apartment in the suburbs to a pizza place in the Lincoln Park area of Chicago. About thirty minutes into the meal, Tom's beeper sounded. He excused himself and spent a long time at the pay phone.

"You're not gonna believe this," Tom announced upon his return, "My best friend's mother just died at dinner and I have to go pick up the body."

I had no idea being a mortician was a twenty-four hour business. Rattled, I suggested that he take me home.

"I don't have time for that," he said as he signaled the waiter for the check and took a last bite of his pizza. "They're waiting for me at the hospital."

"By the way, how did she die?" I asked as he swallowed.

"She choked to death over dinner with her husband." Some omen.

Back at the station wagon, Tom proved to be utterly prepared for his mission. He opened the rear door. Hanging inside was a dark suit, a dark tie, a dark pair of shoes, and a white shirt. Without any hesitation he stepped into the suit, right there in the parking lot. I couldn't believe it and tried not to look. "Boy, if it was anyone but my best friend, I would have someone else do it," Tom said as he zipped his fly. By the time he was finished changing, he looked—just like a mortician. "Ready?" he asked with a professional smile. "Let's go."

The forty-five minute drive to the hospital seemed endless. Strained chatter. No music. When we finally reached the hospital, I was relieved to spot the dazed, mourning family of eight perched on the curb. They all welcomed Tom warmly. That was to be expected; they all knew him. What blew me away was how congenial they were to me. "How many dates have you been on?" they inquired as if I was his steady girlfriend.

"Well, this is the first one," I replied awkwardly.

"Are you having fun?" they asked without a hint of irony. What could I say?

As soon as the family departed, Tom said, "I have to go in and get her. Do you want to come along?" Despite the fact that it was dark, the parking lot was filled with dangerous characters, and I was an experienced nurse, I opted to stay in the station wagon. Ten minutes later the back of the station wagon opened up and this stretcher slid in and rammed up against the back of my seat. How inconsiderate! He could have shoved the dead body in behind his seat. Curious nonetheless, I peeked over my shoulder to see how the nurses prepared the corpse. It was completely enclosed in a white covering with no ropes to hold the stretcher in place.

Tom got back in the car. "O.K. Now what?" I asked.

"Now, we have to take her back up to Lincoln Park to the mortuary." Oh, brother, another forty-five-minute drive!

As we were driving I thought, "How many times have I driven on a freeway? Right now, I'm on a freeway with a dead body over my shoulder that could slide off its stretcher when my date hits the brakes."

"Boy, you're gonna have to tell this story to your grandchildren," Tom said, trying to add a little levity to the situation. Then he pulled into a 7-11 and stopped the car. "I'm going in to get cigarettes."

"Why? You don't smoke."

"No," he chuckled nervously, "but we both will now." And he disappeared into the store, entrusting me to stand guard.

On the cancer ward, even though I tried to be clinical about the task of handling dead bodies, I often had this lingering fear that the person wasn't quite dead; that the body might come back to life before the flesh cooled. Sitting in that car alone with the corpse, I was suddenly overwhelmed with that same creepy feeling. I glanced over my shoulder. Thankfully the "stiff" was still stiff.

Forty-five minutes and several cigarettes later, Tom pulled into his family's funeral home in Lincoln Park. This time I accepted his invitation to come inside. I didn't feel like waiting in a parking lot for the third time in one night.

Tom wheeled the body into the refrigerated section of the mortuary. "Hello," a voice echoed in the dark. I jumped back in terror. It was just the caretaker, but for me it was the last straw. I went numb.

Tom offered to show me what he did with the bodies. He offered me a tour of his family's facility. I couldn't stomach any of it. "Well then," he coughed, "I have a funeral tomorrow. Do you mind if I drive you home in a hearse? It'll save me a trip in the morning." I stifled a giggle. "What's so funny?" he asked. I couldn't believe he didn't know.

The Little Sleep

RICHARD SHERMAN
*Richard is an orthopaedic surgeon
practicing in the Chicago area. He is
married with three children.*

I was on a heavy rotation in medical school and hadn't gone out with a girl in four months. But I was determined to find time for my blind date with the Jewish beauty queen from Northwestern University.

I got up at 4:30 A.M., got to the hospital by 5:30, got all my work done, left the hospital by 6:30 P.M., arrived home at 7:00, called my blind date. "I just got home, got all the work done. I'm really looking forward—Pick you up at 8:00."

She said, "Fine."

At about a quarter to eight I called her. "It's 7:45, I'm leaving my house, I'm not on call, I'll be there in five minutes." I put down the phone, got in my car, drove to her apartment, went in, buzzed the buzzer...There was no answer.

How could that be? I just talked to her. I double checked the address, buzzed the buzzer... Again, no answer.

I looked on the list of names of people in the building and noticed there was someone that I knew from high school on the fourth floor. I buzzed his number. "Can I use your phone?"

I called her and I let the phone ring and ring and ring and ring. Again, no answer.

I got upset. I had changed my whole schedule—including trading in two favors—to get the night off. I couldn't figure out what had happened. I marched back to my car, drove home, called her again. This time she answered.

"Where are you?" she asked.

"What do you mean, where am I?" I snapped. "I've been to your place, I buzzed your buzzer, I called you from someone else's apartment—"

"I must have dozed off," she said groggily.

"How could you doze off?" I asked in amazement. "I just called you five minutes before I left!"

"I don't know... I was sitting here watching TV and I just dozed off."

I thought she had to be lying. How could anybody doze off when they are about to go on a date? Especially to fall into such a deep sleep that you don't hear the doorbell or the phone ring. As far as I was concerned, she should have just stood me up completely or given me a simple "no" on the phone.

She tried to make peace and made a casual offer to go out another night. I said, "Listen, I get your message loud and clear!" And I hung up.

My friends couldn't believe my response. "You're crazy, she's so beautiful, she's so this, she's so that . . . " But I was humiliated. How could I go out with a girl who was so unenthusiastic about dating me that she fell into a deep sleep five minutes after I told her I would be by to pick her up? I had my pride.

About two years later, I ran into a doctor friend of mine at a medical convention who insisted on telling me a wild story. "I had the weirdest experience last night," the doctor said. "I went out with a gal. We were eating dinner and right in the middle of a sentence, her eyes closed and her head dropped down into her soup. Into a full bowl of soup! I didn't know if she'd had a seizure or a cerebral aneurysm or died. I lifted up her face and wiped it off and suddenly she came to."

"You're kidding," I laughed. "She probably had narcolepsy."

"That's exactly what she had," he stated very seriously. Narcolepsy is a sleeping disorder that causes a person to fall into a deep sleep at the drop of a hat.

"Who was she?" I asked, still chuckling at the image of his date's head in a bowl of noodles.

The doctor told me his date's name and I stopped laughing. It was the Jewish beauty queen from Northwestern University who blew off our date two years before. Poor girl. She was telling me the truth, that she had fallen asleep five minutes after I had called, and I thought she didn't care.

Night of the Dentist

HILARY LARKIN
*Hilary is a mother of two who lives
in Yorktown Heights, New York.
She works as a bookkeeper at a
medical center and waitresses
two nights a week.*

The divorced dentist was about twelve years older than I was. A Rotary man. And this was ladies' night at the Rotary club. It was an annual event for two hundred at the Hotel Thayer, a big, fancy, old establishment on the campus of West Point. I had visions of being a princess that night in my sophisticated Wedgwood blue gown with the lace jacket that my mother and I had spent quite a long time trying to find. My mother had visions of me marrying the dentist. She knew I was already crazy about his big green eyes, his brown moustache, and the obviously mischievous look on his face.

The dashing dentist picked me up in a large '73 Cadillac with his mother in tow. (It was ladies' night for all ages, I learned.) The mother, who never liked me, wasn't the problem with the evening. The problem was his friends. I don't know if it was the generation gap or what, but I thought his friends were doing weird things for people their age. One pregnant woman was dancing around the dance floor like an idiot. Others were getting drunk and acting crazy. I put some of them down. I criticized the out-of-date music. Unfortunately, no amount of pouting seemed to get the dentist to pay any attention to me. He was Mr. Partier, the center of attention, the one everybody loved. Finally, I got so annoyed I asked if I could leave. He said, "Sure take my Cadillac. Go on, leave."

As I was making my way to the car my date suddenly swooped down on me, scooped me up (I'm only 5'2"), dumped me into the trunk of the car, shut the hood, and drove off. I couldn't believe it. This wasn't a bar where drunk guys toss around their girlfriends. This was a formal affair on a military campus!

I panicked, thinking, "This is an old car. The exhaust is probably faulty. You can't smell carbon monoxide fumes. I'm going to die in the trunk of his Cadillac in my lovely blue gown."

I banged on the trunk. He continued to drive. I banged harder. He drove faster. I banged again. The movement stopped. It was dark and quiet. Then a man's voice said, "Don't worry, ma'am. We'll get you out of there. Buddy, open up."

"You can open it if you want," the dentist retorted, "but I'm not letting her out!"

I waited in silence for the stalemate to break, then I heard some keys jingling. The trunk opened and I found myself staring up into the faces of my mildly embarrassed date, another confused member of the Rotary Club, a busload of curious people, and a stern West Point checkpoint guard.

The guard detained us for some time, trying to verify if I knew my abductor. I considered lying but figured it wouldn't be too great for his dental practice.

As soon as the interrogation was over, I split. No question about it, I was walking home alone! He followed alongside me in the Caddy. "You want a ride?" he asked flirtatiously. I was crazy in love with him and said, "Oh, all right," then jumped in the car and off we went. I guess I liked the fact that he didn't want to put up with me when I was being a little brat.

Although we didn't speak to each other the whole way home, the evening had been exciting enough for both of us to want to see each other again. We did so for quite some time. Eventually we realized we would kill each other if we stayed together, so we went our separate ways. He married a schoolteacher and I married an Englishman. As a result, I'm now very quiet and reserved.

Cat Scratch Fever

MICHELLE BARRY
*Michelle is an accountant in the
San Francisco Bay Area. After this date,
she began to study karate.*

When my fiancé of two years broke my heart and moved out of our condo in San Mateo, I was anxious to have a date and show him, "Yeah, I've got someone already!" So, I was probably a little too trusting when I accepted a sweet invitation from the computer programmer who lived four doors down to come over for pizza and a drink.

I was a bit surprised to find him drunk when I arrived for our date. However, my antennae were so off from two years in a relationship and a devastated heart, I didn't notice much at first. It was only later that I realized what a strange drunk he was.

He told me that he wrote a lot of programs for accountants and he wanted to know if I could explain some basic accounting concepts to him. He thought it could improve his work. I slipped home and picked up my accounting books. When I returned he offered me a beer while he sipped a half-empty bottle of vodka. He never mentioned the pizza he promised, although I did notice it thawing on the kitchen counter. We began the lesson with his comment, "Please go at a basic level, so I'm sure I understand it." I started doing just that and within a few minutes he suddenly turned on me. "You're patronizing me. Don't talk down to me!" Whoaaa! I slammed the books closed and said, "O.K., let's change the subject."

We then began to talk about his beautiful condo. It was an end unit with nice furnishings and plants. He told me he planned to move into a small studio apartment in San Francisco. "I have too much furniture here," he noted. "Really what I ought to do is give it to some friends. But," he muttered, looking down at the floor, "I don't have any friends." O.K., another depressing topic. Let's change the subject.

We then moved on to cats. My cats, Bonsai and Escrow. "I want your cats to come over here," he announced. "I think your cats should be as comfortable in my condo as they are in yours." I tried to ignore his suggestion, hoping to coax him into baking the pizza, but he became adamant. "Go get the cats."

"I don't think that's a good idea, they've never been out of the condo except to visit the vet and they'll just be scared and run under the couch."

"No. I really want your cats to come over here."

"But you don't have a litter box and they could have an accident."

"I want your cats!"

"You have a lot of beautiful houseplants here and my cats eat plants."

"I want your cats here! Now!"

Whoaa. At this point in my life, I was so emotionally shell-shocked, I actually thought *I* must be doing something wrong here. I rationalized, if I just brought the cats, it would calm him down and I could get through the evening.

I went down the hall, got the cats, came back and just as I predicted, they ran under the couch. He started chasing them around, crying, "Here kitty, kitty, kitty." They didn't come out. He said, "Well, if I feed them, they'll like me. What do they eat?"

"They're not gonna eat. They're very scared. They don't eat when they're scared."

My response didn't phase him. "I want to feed them. They will like me. What will they eat?"

"O.K., O.K., O.K.," I said trying to deflect his anger. "Why don't you just give them lunch meat?"

"Yes. Yes." So he ran into the kitchen, opened the fridge, pulled out this bologna loaf, tore it up, and chased the cats around calling, "Here kitty, kitty, kitty," as he waved the lunch meat in front of their faces. They, of course, would have none of this. Disgusted, he retreated to the kitchen and threw the bologna down on the floor. Then he marched back into the living room, pulled Bonsai out from under the couch by his paws, dragged him into the kitchen, and shoved his face in the meat. The cat just hunched and fled.

"That was my lunch for the week," he screamed. "They didn't like lunch meat. Now I have nothing to eat for the week!" (As if he were really that poor.)

"I'm really sorry," I replied. "I don't know what to say. Maybe we should change the subject..."

As was I speaking, I noticed Escrow starting to munch on his houseplants. He noticed it too. "That's it!" he declared triumphantly, "Why did you tell me to give them lunch meat? It's greens they want!"

With that, he ran into the kitchen, found some lettuce, tore it up, and threw it on the floor. Then he dashed back out to the living room, got the cat, carried him back to the kitchen, and shoved his face in the shredded lettuce. Of course Escrow wouldn't touch the lettuce. He only liked houseplants!

He tried to force Escrow to swallow the lettuce. Escrow fought to get away. Finally, I couldn't endure the struggle any more. I scooped up Escrow, retrieved Bonsai from under the couch, told him that I had to go, and ran down the hall. He stood there, not saying anything as I slammed the door to my condo and locked it. Luckily, he didn't come after me. However, for the next month, whenever I left my apartment, I would peek out and make sure he wasn't there.

The moral of the story is really quite simple. Don't take cats on a date, don't go out with men in your building, and don't consider dating when your antennae aren't functioning normally.

All Washed Up

DIANA YURKOVIC

*Diana is a publishing manager for
a children's book company. She grew
up in Los Angeles, but now lives in
Denver with her two children.*

The senior prom was coming up and I'd just gotten my braces off. I looked great but I didn't have a date. My lab partner in chemistry, Steve, had already asked me to go, but I hadn't given him an answer. That's because I was really holding out for this new guy in my English class. With him on my arm, everything would be so perfect and so cool.

Then a miracle happened. Eric Johns, the good-looking prepster with the brown cowlick—the upper crust, Santa Monica boy who owned an entire collection of the Harvard Classics—asked me to the prom. I said yes right away.

Eric suggested that we go on a "pre-prom" date, so if we didn't hit it off, he wouldn't have to shell out all that money for one night. I agreed. We decided to go out on a Sunday since that was the only day I had off from my after-school job at the Big Boy Dog Kennels. He was going to take me to a polo match at Will Rogers State Park.

On Sunday morning the surf was up, so my brother and I went surfing early like we had done since I was eight. Although I was a lame surfer, I kept at it because it was the key to a popularity of sorts growing up in Malibu.

That day I got clobbered by some huge waves and swallowed a gallon of water, but I had fun anyway. When we finally returned to the house, I only had enough time to shower and change before Eric came by to pick me up. His parents were already waiting for us at the polo field.

Eric's parents had an elaborate picnic lunch spread out for us with elegant china dishes and crystal glasses. There were classy finger sandwiches and ripe fruit, smelly cheese, and a beautiful carrot cake. I was a little nervous, but Eric's dad was nice to me and his mom offered me a glass of real champagne. I felt like such an adult, sitting there drinking "bubbly" and watching the match.

After a while Mrs. Johns asked me if I might like a sandwich. I said I would. But when I leaned forward to take the sandwich, I felt a sudden, sharp stinging in my sinuses and a huge stream of seawater started pouring out of my nose right onto the carrot cake. I panicked and tried to cover my face. Unfortunately my nose was like a spigot that wouldn't shut off. The cascading water soon formed a small dam of cream cheese carrots on the surface of the ruined dessert.

Eric and his parents watched me, frozen. They weren't beachy types and didn't know this was a common problem for surfers, although rarely this embarrassing or extreme. Eventually Mrs. Johns pulled the cake away and sniffed, "Well."

I couldn't respond with a simply apology; I was twisting around, blushing from embarrassment and holding my breath, dreading what was to come next.

I farted. It was audible. There was no connection between the emissions. Just bad timing.

Dead silence, dead romance, dead rest of the day. Eric's dad dropped me off at home and I went to the prom with my lab partner.

Based on an interview with and a story
by Diana Yurkovic.

Mr. Clean

SUSAN MEHRTENS

Susan owns and operates a business teaching pre-kindergarten. She lives in Baton Rouge, Louisiana, and has two children.

Phil was so determined to worm his way into my life that he started a rumor that we were going steady. Nothing could have been further from the truth. It didn't matter to me that he looked like a fifteen-year-old Michael Landon (with acne). I was a tenth grade cheerleader in Memphis, Tennessee, and I wasn't about to be seen with a boy my own age.

My mother was very uncomfortable with my position because, in her mind, older boys were drinking and smoking pot and had long hair. I had dated one who was five years my senior and there had been a car accident. As a result, my mother felt the need to protect me.

Phil was a very smart young man and instantly deduced that the way to get to me was through my mother. Just before Christmas, he started coming around to my house.

He helped my mother decorate the Christmas tree. He petted the dog and volunteered to bathe it.

He even waxed enthusiastic about the Bing Crosby Christmas records my mother was playing, though no one else my age could stand them. Sure enough, mother invited Phil to stay for dinner.

At dinner, he didn't just eat. He had two or three servings of everything. "Oh this is the best food I've ever eaten!" You would have thought he was a motherless child! My mother is an intelligent woman, but she was just lapping it up. I was dying. Phil then asked my mother (not me!) if it would be all right if he took me to the drive-in on Saturday night. "My brother, who's in the service, and his wife will chaperone us. We can have Susan in by midnight, will that be all right?"

My mother beamed, "Oh, Susan loves the drive-in!"

I sat there with my fork in my mashed potatoes thinking, "To the drive-in? Jesus! Now she wants a guy to whisk me off in his Firebird and take advantage of me!"

As soon as Phil left I begged my mother to reconsider. "Why?" she asked. "He's a nice boy. He's willing to spend time with the family and what's wrong with that?" I knew it was useless. There was only one way to do things in our family—her way.

When they came to the door to pick me up, the brother and his pregnant wife came in first. As Phil had done, the brother shook my father's hand and petted the dog. "We'll keep a close eye on them, sir," he assured my father. "Should she be in earlier than midnight?" I looked at Momma. She was almost crowing. She knew she'd found the perfect man for me. But I still had this feeling there was something wrong.

While we were making small talk in the car, I asked Phil's brother's wife how old she was. She said she was seventeen and expecting twins. Right then I realized that my chaperone was not the family man my mother thought. Theirs had been a shotgun wedding for sure.

As soon as we parked at the drive-in, the boys pulled an ice chest out from under the seat. It contained several eight-ounce Tupperware tumblers full of pre-mixed screwdrivers. They all started drinking like fish—even the pregnant wife!

Phil drank to impress me. He drank to compete with his brother. He drank and he drank and he drank. By time the movie was over, Phil was numb drunk.

His brother started driving. Phil rolled the window down on his side of the back seat and started hollering every cuss word he'd ever heard at passing cars. Some drivers gave us the finger. Others ignored us. The brother added to the chaos by throwing smoke bombs and screaming "Fire!" It was a rowdy, rolling party until we stopped for a red light.

Then Phil urinated on the car next to us. That set the brother off. He cursed Phil for potentially causing trouble and drove straight back to his apartment to sober Phil up. My curfew was fast approaching and big brother knew Phil couldn't face my mother in his current condition.

Big Brother's method for getting rid of drunkenness was not something we normally use here in the South. He poured dishwashing liquid, mixed with a little water and a raw egg, down poor Phil's throat. Did he throw up?! He tried to make it to the bathroom, but wasn't fast enough. So he threw up all through the living room and down the hall.

When he was finished vomiting, Phil threw a punch at his brother. The punch escalated into a fistfight, which escalated into knocking holes in a bedroom dresser and damaging walls. (If only Mom could see Mr. Perfect now!) At that point I realized I should have called my parents and warned them I'd be late, but I wasn't sure which would be worse, their wrath or this.

The fighting went on another fifteen minutes until the drunken siblings wore each other out. Phil announced he was going to be sick again and needed to go to the bathroom. Big Brother thought he was bluffing, but reluctantly agreed to let him go. A few minutes later, Phil emerged from the bathroom buck naked, and raced out of the house. He ran down the street toward Madison Avenue, one of the main streets for nightlife in Memphis.

His brother dashed after him. The pregnant wife ran out onto the front lawn, holding her belly.

I stood there with my hands over my mouth and watched as several other neighbors joined in the chase. The last thing I saw was Phil's bare behind disappearing into the darkness.

Soon, big brother returned with Phil. He was scraped up and bloody, with embedded gravel and abrasions in some very unseemly places. "He hit me...with a car!" he cried out. "He didn't just hit me, he hit me with a car!"

The brother knew my curfew was up. We had to go. He forced Phil into his blue jeans and we drove off.

Poor Phil. The movement of the car made him sick again. This time he threw up in the vehicle. I hugged up against my side to avoid the spray.

When we pulled up in front of our house, my mother pounced on that car like a chicken on a bug. She flung the door open and surveyed the damage. Phil was bleeding, half-naked, and still vomiting. The car reeked.

Two nights later, Phil came by my house and made a peace offering of a ring with a diamond chip. He still wanted to go steady. My mother felt so betrayed and humiliated, she didn't want me to speak to him. But I felt I should. I told him I couldn't take the ring or see him any more. He started to cry, "Can't you just give me another chance?" You would have thought we were in a relationship for twelve years!

I've always wondered what happened to Phil after high school. Maybe he joined the service like his brother and continued to drink like a fish. Or maybe he turned to dishwashing liquid.

Expanded from an original story by Susan Mehrtens.

Blood Is Thicker than Ice Cream

ROBERT SIMONSON

*Robert is a restaurant cashier who
lives in Connecticut. He has a B.A. in
German, Mensa status, and is still
single and eternally optimistic.*

Joanne and I hit it off when we talked at the deli
department of my local Grand Union grocery
store. She worked there; I was a frequent customer. It seemed natural enough to ask her out.
She had a good sense of humor, a nice smile, and a
full body.

One night we went out to the Friendly Ice
Cream shop for a simple dinner. She was in the
middle of telling me about her nephew Raymond
when he and his skinny, blonde, eighteen-year-old
girlfriend sauntered in. Raymond had left his parents out in New Mexico and had moved in with his
aunt—my date, Joanne—because she was easier to
live with. He seemed to be a typical teenaged mis-
fit—6'4", long black hair, moustache. He looked
like he ought to be in a rock band, but in reality he
hadn't really found a niche.

He and his groupie-type girlfriend sat and chatted with us for about half an hour. Minor conversation. Nothing memorable. Then they split and I never saw them again. Joanne and I continued our date for another half an hour, and then we left. Soon, she was transferred to another Grand Union up in Milford and I never got around to asking her out again.

Six months later, I was reading the newspaper and I saw Joanne's name on the front page. It turned out that Raymond had a jealous ex-girlfriend who didn't want to let him go. The girl had evidently been such a pest that Joanne, Raymond, and the blonde decided that the only way to get rid of her was to kill her. One night Joanne drove Ms. Ex to a designated spot in the woods where Raymond was supposed to meet her. Joanne left her there. Raymond showed up and engaged Ms. Ex. in a conversation. Then the blonde snuck up behind her and strangled her with a length of wire. Apparently Raymond and the blonde went at it after that.

The girl was killed. They stripped her body, took whatever they could, buried her under some brush, then all drove back to Milford, shared a pizza, and joked about it. Evidently they had bragged a little too much about their antics in the woods because someone turned them in. The cops had already found the body—which had been reported missing for days—and they were already under suspicion. It was front-page news for the next couple of days.

I always thought Joanne had more sense than that, but blood is thicker than water, I guess. Joanne was sentenced to ten years in prison as an accomplice to murder. Raymond and the blonde got about twenty.

To this day, the thought of that date is very creepy. We've all had the experience of discovering unexpected facts about the people we date—they have another boyfriend or they have bad habits—but you never suspect they'll be an accomplice to murder.

A Low Encounter with His Highness

MARIA DEMBICKI
*Born in Russia, Maria lived in
England where she was a member of
the Womens Royal Naval Service.
She moved to the U.S. in 1951,
had three children, and is now
working on her memoirs.*

My father, a major in the Intelligence Corps in World War II, had met Stanislav Radzewil, a Polish prince who had just escaped and was planning to set up a government in exile. My father thought he would be the perfect date for me. Knowing of my distaste for noblemen of any sort, he didn't tell me about the arrangement until we were on our way to meet the man at the Polonia Restaurant, a fairly fancy club in otherwise bombed-out London. I was a twenty-five-year-old member of the Womens Royal Naval Service at the time and often came down to visit my recently widowed father for weekends.

When we arrived at the restaurant with military punctuality, we found the prince was nowhere

in sight. "His Highness is late," the maître d'
informed us, "but he instructed us to seat you at
his table." Our party—my father with his lady
friend, myself, a lady officer from the MI5/SHAEF,
and her fiancé—sat down and waited.

Eventually, a curtain parted and the prince
appeared. There was a flurry of bowing and scrap-
ing and grandiose waving to the public, then His
Highness was ushered to our table. As he slowly
approached, I scrutinized him. He was an unim-
posing little man with a waxed, curled moustache.
He was in his forties, flabby, and somewhat
droopy at the shoulders. He wore a black suit, gray
suede spats, and white gloves, and sported a monocle in the right eye. His dark hair, flecked with
gray, was parted in the middle and smarmed down
with so much brilliantine I was afraid it might drip
down onto anyone beside him. I was a good looking, 100-pound gal at the time who wasn't at all
desperate for a man. "My God," I thought, "does
my father want me to date *that*?!"

Everybody at our table jumped up and stood
to attention—except for me. I didn't want to rise
for this oaf. But my father grabbed my elbow and
forced me up.

My father and the other officers clicked their
heels and bowed. The prince shook hands with
them, then looked at the ladies. My father's lady
friend dropped curtsy in a very royal manner, bow-

ing her head. The prince took her right hand in his gloved hand and kissed his own thumb! Next, the lady officer curtsied, copying my father's lady friend, and again the prince took her hand and kissed his thumb.

It was my turn—my father grabbed me by the shoulder and pushed me forward, saying, "This is my little girl."

I shot my father a dirty look, then turned to the prince, stared him right in the eyes, and defiantly refused to curtsy or extend my hand. "I bow down for no man but God alone himself," I declared haughtily.

"Ho, ho," said the prince. "I like a spirited girl. I think we'll have a lot of fun taming you!"

The party went on merrily in spite of my bad behavior. Lots of vodka and other drinks were consumed by everyone but me. Soon, the music started up and his Highness asked me to dance. I refused. He insisted, "But your papa tells me that you're an excellent dancer!"

I sniffed, "Maybe I am, but with the right partner."

Horrified, my father whisked me onto the dance floor and gave me an awful telling off, "You will do as I tell you tonight and dance with the prince." I couldn't protest any further because the prince literally dragged me away. I made myself limp, like a Raggedy Ann doll, forcing His

Highness to carry my dead weight. He threw me down, "You are a feisty wench!"

"I am," I replied, "and you're a disgusting filthy person."

Suddenly, the old familiar air raid siren wailed. Lights went out and we all dove under the tables. Almost immediately there was a loud explosion and tremor. Something was hit close by.

The instant we were under our table, the prince grabbed hold of me and started unbuttoning my uniform shirt. I struggled the best I could in the crowded confines and then hauled off and slapped him with such a loud whack that everybody in the whole room could hear it. "Somebody's being naughty," my father snickered.

Within minutes the "all clear" sounded. The lights came on and people emerged from under the tables. I appeared, buttoning up my shirt and swearing like a trooper, followed by the prince, who now sported a bright red imprint of my whole hand on his cheek and no monocle! I spied it and quickly ground it into the wooden floor with the heel of my heavy service shoe. Undaunted, he reached into his inside breast pocket with a theatrical flourish and quipped, "Never mind my dear, there's plenty more where that came from." With that, he produced another monocle, inserted it in his right eye with a terrible grimace, rubbed the red imprint, and stomped off to an empty booth nearby. Seconds later, a couple of adolescent American girls, wearing bobby socks and cooing "Oh, poor Prince," climbed on his knee and kissed him.

As luck would have it, I married a Polish soldier. A few years later, when I was in my eighth month of pregnancy, I learned that the prince was having a reception. He had formed an interim government in exile and wanted to meet his loyal subjects. All the Polish emigrés and soldiers who were in England at the time signed up to meet him. I didn't want to go but my husband insisted it would help our strapped financial condition.

We appeared at the White Eagle Club in London on the appointed day and time and stood in a slow-moving line to be formally presented to the prince. While we waited, I scrutinized him once again: he was wearing a formal morning coat with gray striped trousers, gray suede spats, and white gloves. His hair was longer now and had a lot more gray in it. He still wore it parted down the center with a lot of brilliantine and he still sported the monocle. The waxed moustache, however, had been replaced by a Van Dyke beard.

When we reached the prince, it was déjà vu. My husband clicked his heels and bowed. The prince shook his hand. Then the prince took in my bloated body with a disgusted look. I didn't move. "Excuse me, Your Highness," I said with a beatific smile, "but in my present condition, it wouldn't be wise if I curtsied." He blinked and asked for my name. I gave it to him in Polish. It didn't seem to register so he simply waved me on.

Before we had time to sample the enticing finger foods, two footmen accosted me, "His Highness wishes a word with you." My husband started to twitter and shake, "Don't tell him anything!"

"Why not?" I scoffed.

The prince had stationed himself away from the crowd in a little alcove of a bay window. I was thrust before him. He eyed me coldly, "Haven't we met before somewhere?"

"Oh, yes indeed," I replied. "Under the table in the Polonia—"

I never had time to finish the sentence. He just snapped his fingers and his footmen appeared. They grabbed me by the elbows and escorted me rapidly through the reception hall. "To what do I owe this very unchivalrous behavior?" I asked as they were about to throw me out on the street.

One of the footmen replied, "Ladies in your condition do not come to formal receptions, only sluts do!" With that they tossed me on the ground.

Based on an interview and an edited excerpt from Maria Dembicki's unpublished manuscript, *Just Mookie, Diary of Adventures and Misadventures of a Jenny Wren.*

A Tough Act to Follow

JEFFREY RESSNER
Jeffrey is a writer and a reporter.

I used to work at a daily paper with a sweet British woman who told me I was a kindred spirit with her sister, Davidia, and would probably hit it off with her. As luck would have it, Davidia was coming in from England for a few days to visit. I wasn't looking for a girlfriend, but I had some faith in my colleague's judgment.

I was never much for blind dates, having gone through a couple of hellish experiences while attending high school in New Jersey. In those days, I'd talk to someone on the phone and we'd be on the same wavelength, but when we'd finally meet in person it would be a disaster. But when Davidia walked into a tea shop where she and her sister set up this rendezvous, it was as if I was hit by a thunderbolt.

Davidia was amazing—every bit the soulful and singular woman her sister had described. We talked for an hour or so; the conversation ranged from John Huston movies to romantic poetry, from pagan religious rites to punk rock guitarists. We discussed morality. We discussed mortality.

Our conversation sped up as we discovered how much we had in common. Within the course of the afternoon we talked about all the heavy things you don't really speak about with most people until you've known them a long, long time, if at all.

Besides her gift for words, Davidia was just bewitching—a distressed goddess, to quote Henry Chinaski. She had aquiline features and high cheekbones, but didn't look like some haughty model or bimbo. Her auburn hair brushed gently against her perfect, almost porcelain skin, and she drew me in even deeper as I got lost in her mystical, seductive eyes.

As we talked, her sister joined us and the three of us went off in their car to a concert. We were going to see Leonard Cohen, a melancholy but brilliant singer-songwriter whose razor-sharp songs are filled with emotion and passion. I had gotten these three tickets figuring that if Davidia and I didn't hit it off, at least I could hang out and talk with her sister. I also thought it would be a nice thing to do.

We got to the concert and it was a killer show. Everything was going so well, it was hard to believe. Then, in the middle of the fifth or sixth song, I noticed that Davidia seemed quite moved by the performance. During a really depressing refrain, I saw a teardrop roll down the side of her face.

At intermission, her sister went to get a cup of coffee in the lobby and we stayed in the theater to talk. I turned to Davidia and we spoke for a few moments about how great the show was. I said, "I guess you were really touched during some of the songs."

She nodded, then confessed she and Leonard Cohen once had an incredibly intense affair that had ended rather strangely. "Would you mind," she asked, "if I went backstage after the show so I could speak with him?"

Suddenly, her sister came back to the aisle and all three of us started chitchatting again. I had to excuse myself and go out to the lobby, where I began to laugh out loud. It was too surreal.

Pretty in Pink

NANCY BRYANT

Nancy Bryant grew up in a town
with one stoplight. She now
works in Los Angeles.

Oh God, this is a weird one. I met this guy a couple of times out clubbing. Actually, a particular
girlfriend of mine, Tammy—who is like a little
"sweet" (still changes in front of the girls with all
her clothes on)—picked him out.

He was like the All-American Boy.
Completely! I mean, blonde hair, brown eyes,
dressed to the hilt. He was from Texas. Around
twenty-eight years old. All my friends, even my
gay-guy friends, were like, "He's soooo cute!" And
on and on. And so we went out.

There were a few other couples with us, and
we were drinking and having a good time and running around, and my date kept on whispering in
my ear all night about his sexual fantasy. "You
gonna live my sexual fantasy?" With this little
Texas twangy thing going on. Kind of teasing me.

I was like, "Yeah, yeah, sure." Because I was a
little buzzed, and I thought, "*Your* sexual fantasy?
Right."

We went back to his house and we were hanging out. Then he looked at me like real seriously and said, "Do you want to hear it now?" By that time, I was ready to go to sleep so I said, "Well, you know, whatever." Then he told me he wanted to put on a pink garter belt and pink lipstick.

"You wanna *what*?"

He wanted to wear *his* pink garter belt for me and put on *his* pink lipstick.

I just said, "I think I will go to sleep now." Kinda putting it off. But I was thinking, this guy looks like someone you'd see in *GQ*. You'd never imagine, you know, "this" from a nice little Texas boy. I figured he probably grew up in a town like Delano where I did—the grape capital of the world—where heavy make out was about as far as you could go without the whole town knowing about it.

A few days later, one of my friends started talking about him and I said, "Ohhh, you know him, too, huh?"

She said, "Yes. He's kind of strange."

I nodded, "Yeah, I know."

She said, "You know what he wanted to do for my girlfriend?"

"Wear a pink garter belt and put on pink lipstick?"

"How did you know?"

So apparently he's been doing this around town a bit. With his looks, with all the weird people in Los Angeles—as kinky as they are—I'm sure he found someone who's into it.

But I don't know about his office. Some time after that, another guy who works for the same company had been calling me and then I found out he was married. I said, "You know, I heard you're married." He said, "Yeah. Want to talk to my wife? We'll both come pick you up." They both wanted to take me home and they both worked at the same office that he does, the pink garter belt guy! I don't know if this is normal behavior for L.A. or just what's required if you work at that company.

Redneck Romeo and Me

ELIZABETH SUTOR
*Elizabeth is a singer-songwriter
who lives in Delaware and performs
along the East Coast. She's still
single and dating.*

According to my girlfriend, Billy had a bad history with women. I'd had a bad marriage, a bad divorce, and bad relationships, and was well on the road to becoming a hermit. "All he wants is a good woman that he can be there for," my girlfriend informed me. "And that's what you need— a nice, nurturing person. Besides, he's adorable and he knows how to cook." Since her husband looked like Jim Palmer and this guy Billy worked for him as a chef, I thought it would all be okay.

A few days later Billy, the chef, called me and asked me to dinner. I was charmed by his Louisiana accent and hoped he would be as attractive as his voice.

About forty-five minutes after he was supposed to have picked me up, a decrepit blue van sputtered into my driveway. A 5'3", two-hundred-pound man jumped out. He was swarthy and severely walleyed. Under what dark light did my girlfriend see him? I promised myself I wouldn't be superficial and reject Billy on the spot. I'd just tough it out.

We climbed into the van, which only had one seat. I sat on a crate, clutching the dashboard, as we chugged down the street. A quarter of a mile down the highway, the van died. Thinking he was out of gas, Billy lumbered off to find a service station. While he was gone, a cop pulled up and gave me the third degree. A serial murderer had been stalking the Wilmington, Delaware area for the past few months and the police were stumped. The only thing connecting the crimes was a blue van. And here I was, all dressed up, sitting in this ratty, blue van with Louisiana plates in the middle of the Delaware highway on a dark night! The suspicious officer wasn't about to budge until I convinced him that I wasn't going to be serial victim number four. "My date is a gentleman who will be back soon," I assured him. What a mistake!

The van failed two more times in the next half hour, depositing us in a remote area next to the local air force base. Billy's cousin and his trashy girlfriend rescued us in a pickup truck. Right then I offered to call it a night, but Billy insisted he could borrow a car from another cousin named Roy so that we could continue the evening.

The first cousin dropped us off in front of a seedy motel in a rough section of town. I expressed some concern about the fact that the place was known to be frequented by hookers, bikers, and other unsavory types. Billy told me not to worry. His aunt was the owner and he lived there with his little sister.

"Oh this place came furnished," I remarked as I walked into his tasteless abode.

"No, no, I did it myself," he said proudly. "Decorating is my hobby."

The room was full of hideous erotic sculpture. Some pieces functioned as lamp bases. Others were three feet high and freestanding. The rest littered the end tables and the coffee table. Thank God they weren't illuminated.

Complementing this, he had a velvet Elvis on the wall, which he actually thought was hot, and a velvet toreador stabbing a bull to death, with little drops of blood oozing out. The furniture was this ersatz Mediterranean stuff—plush and gaudy. Hanging between the rooms were multi-colored bead curtains like the ones you might have seen in a late '60s Peter Fonda movie. It was truly appalling.

The only nice item in the place was an old pencil sketch that was mounted on a wall. The subject was a forty-year-old woman. "That's a lovely drawing," I noted. "When was it done? The '50s?"

"That's my mother," Billy replied. "We did it last year for her birthday."

For her birthday? He was only twenty-seven. I was thirty-eight. Had I run smack into an Oedipus complex? You bet. "Momma was a saint," he offered without prompting. "You just don't know what she had to put up with. She held the whole family together. She had it really rough after Daddy died. She'd been so perfect and so pure ... "

"That's terrible, Billy," I said sympathetically, "What happened to your father?"

"Momma shot him," he replied matter-of-factly, then retreated to the kitchen because he'd decided to cook.

Two seconds later the front door flew open and this size sixteen creature barged in. She'd shoehorned herself into a pair of size nine jeans, a black tank top, and a set of spike-heeled black boots. She had a tattoo on her shoulder and pitch-black hair, the best that L'Oréal could offer. I thought, "Oh no, his disgruntled lover has come to cut me into ribbons."

But as it turned out, baby sister had finally come home from walking on Route 273, which is where the hookers like to stroll. She claimed she wasn't one in those spike-heeled boots, thank you very much, and was only going to stay for a while because she wanted to go back out and find the fun guy she'd slept with the night before, even though she couldn't remember his name and didn't know where he might be. Whoa!

She then started telling me how she'd come up here to stop the wedding. According to Sis, Billy had had an *older wife*, Tammy, who died, and on the rebound, he married *this other gal* named Jean. That didn't work out either. Then, a few years ago, when he was twenty-five, Billy had *a fiancée in her forties* named Barbara who died in a terrible car accident they had been in together. I did not find out who was driving. Several days after that, *their son* died. To get over those two shocking deaths, Billy moved up here to Delaware to stay with his aunt and find work as a chef. In Delaware, he met *another older woman* named Louise, and they were married and divorced in the space of three weeks. Baby Sister had come up north to stop the wedding but it was too late. "Louise just wanted him for his money!" she groused. With that van and this apartment, what money could she be talking about?

At that moment, Cousin Roy pulled up out front. Billy told Baby Sister to go outside and ask Roy to lend him his car. After a brother-sister screamfest, she reluctantly complied, then took off in search of last night's lover. That left Billy and me alone to enjoy his home-cooked, white-on-white meal. An odd choice for a professional chef.

As soon as dinner was over, Billy became amorous. He flopped down on the sofa in what could only be considered an inviting pose. God forbid! Rejected, he grabbed the remote and clicked through every channel cable had to offer, while babbling on about mom. What a saint she was. How Poppa had sexually and physically abused all her children. That's why Momma shot him. Momma went to jail, but they got her out. It was such a bad soap opera, it gave me a headache. I told Billy I needed to leave. To his credit, he borrowed the car and took me right home.

Although the date with Billy lasted only four hours, it felt like a full night in hell, co-directed by Fellini and Woody Allen.

Loose-Lipped Lone Star

DON PAYNE
Don is trucker who lives in Texas.

I was hauling oil field equipment up from
Houston to Alaska, a fifteen day round-trip run,
and on the way we'd pass through Odessa, Texas.
There was this girl I'd met up there at the truck
stop I'd been wanting to date for a long time. She
was a dishwater blonde with a coke-bottle figure.
Good lookin' nineteen-year-old gal. At twenty-
one, I wasn't bad looking either. So I asked her out.

Out in west Texas, everybody goes dancing
on Saturday nights. The blonde and I planned to
meet at the Starlight Ballroom around seven-thirty.
Several hundred people came out that night, most
of them in western dress. She was in jeans. I wore
my 5x Beaver brown Stetson. The band was playing western music.

We'd been there a couple of hours. Drank a
few beers. Had a good time. The potential was real
good. We got out on the floor to dance a bop. My
buddy, who's well over 6'1", was getting up a
storm next to us with his girl. He twirled his partner, and when he swung her around, he hit me

113

right in the side of the jaw like he was throwing a punch. My new brown Stetson flew off my head and my false teeth, which I'd gotten a few days earlier, jumped out of my mouth and landed fifteen feet across the floor.

I turned my date loose on the dance floor and hoofed on after my possessions. Back then, it cost about four hundred dollars just for an upper plate like mine. The Stetson was worth another seventy or eighty bucks.

I'd seen where the teeth hit, but I couldn't catch 'em. Every time I'd try to get 'em somebody would accidentally kick 'em. "Get off my damn teeth," I hollered. Not a soul knew what I was talking about until I hit 'em on the foot. Then, they thought I was crazy. But I kept hitting and fishing and those teeth and that hat kept slipping and sliding. Finally, I got down on my hands and knees.

I must have been crawling around the dance floor getting kicked for five minutes, maybe longer. By the time I caught up with my belongings, the plate had lost a tooth and the Stetson was crushed. My knees were covered with stardust, the corn meal they throw on the dance floor to make things slicker. I looked like a sorry state.

Still keen to continue the date, I cleaned up the denture, went back out to my truck, got some Polygrip and stuck them back in. I explained to my date that I didn't have my teeth that long. They were just getting comfortable enough for me to wear them without hurting my mouth.

We finished the dance that night. Had a pretty good time. Then we went out for something to eat. It was a cool December night and the restaurant was serving one of my favorites, hot potato soup. I took a couple bites of it and she was eating hers. Then that Polygrip let me down once again. It melted—and there went my teeth right in that god dang bowl. My date jumped up from her chair and said, "Huh! That's the last time. I've seen all of them damn teeth I want to see." And that's the last I ever saw of her. She left me sitting there with my teeth in the bowl.

The Lawyer from Arizona

EVE BRANDSTEIN

Eve has worked as a studio executive, a casting executive, a producer, a director, a writer-creator of a TV series, an author, and a poet. She's still single and having bad dates.

"**I**'m not interested in another blind date," I told my girlfriend. "I've already had a string of bad ones: the guy who couldn't stop talking, the guy who wouldn't say a word, the guy who looked at his watch every five minutes, the guy who looked at another girl every five minutes, the guy who brought his child, and the guy who cried."

"This one won't be anything like that," she assured me. "He's attractive, wealthy, successful, and smart."

"What does he do?"

"He's a lawyer from Arizona, but he comes to L.A. often." Even if you cut this description in half, I thought this guy sounded great.

One night several weeks later, I was supposed to go out to a party with my girlfriend and a group of her friends, including, as she put it, "a surprise."

I put two and two together and decided that the surprise must be the lawyer from Arizona.

Three guys I didn't know walked into my girl-friend's apartment. Two of them were nothing to talk about, but one of them was truly gorgeous— as well as masculine and big and sexy. I looked at him and he looked at me and I thought, "Oh God, I hope he's the lawyer from Arizona."

"I'm really tired from my trip to Arizona," he confessed as he was introduced to the group. My heart leaped.

We immediately gravitated towards each other and spent most of the evening just sitting and communicating incredibly well—with his hand pressed gently on top of mine. We talked about relationships—why they don't work and how he really wanted one. We talked about love and chil-dren, about men and women. I thought, this man is one of the most sensitive lawyers I have ever met. Where did he come from?

Then it occurred to me that somehow in all of our conversation, we'd missed exchanging vital statistics like age, education, and so forth. So I said to him, "Tell me a little about your work."

"As you know, I'm an actor... "

The moment I heard that word, it was as if my hand was attacked by fire. I pulled it away very aggressively and shouted, "You're not an actor, you're a lawyer!"

"What are you talking about?"

"Then what were you doing in Arizona?" I demanded.

"I was on location. What's the matter?"

I looked down and finally, after a long pause, squeaked, "I'm a casting director."

He started laughing, "What's wrong with that?"

"There's nothing wrong with that," I said sadly. "But you're supposed to be a lawyer from Arizona."

Later that evening, I tried scolding my girl-friend. "You know I don't date actors. It's unprofessional."

"You could have picked the stockbroker, Eve, but you had to go for the one who was attractive."

"Well, what happened to the lawyer from Arizona?"

"He got married."

The Desired Mix of Warmth and Sarcasm

EVAN COHEN

*Evan is an attorney who specializes
in music, copyright laws, and
related litigation.*

For some reason, my girlfriend chose to demand an end to our brief but emotionally draining affair on the final night of my bar exam. Hoping to get a fresh start, I called a certain nineteen-year-old named Megan, who I believed possessed the desired mix of warmth and sarcasm, and invited her to go to the latest itinerant downtown dance club, the Dirtbox.

Things started to go awry a scant half hour after my initial telephone call. It seemed that the friend who had introduced us, Randi, had been involved in a frightening car wreck, and although aching, was wondering if she might join the two of us for the evening. To this day, I have no idea what being in an auto accident has to do with wanting to go out dancing until all hours of the night. At any rate, not wanting to appear to be less than a sport, I agreed to pick up both Megan and Randi in the Valley.

After assuring Megan's conventional parents that, unlike her other somewhat dubious boyfriends, I had indeed taken the bar exam, we left her house, picked up a sedate (and probably sedated) Randi, and headed downtown to the land of warehouses, dirty cement floors, and cheap beer.

The English expatriate who was manning the door that night did not like my haircut. After rather speedy negotiations we entered the club. For the next hour or so I was genuinely trying to have a good time by drinking Budweiser, dancing, and exchanging pleasantries with my date. I then realized I had made an unfortunate choice of venue, for right in the middle of a rather pleasing and upbeat number, I looked up and saw my ex-girlfriend, with a date, dancing not fifteen feet from me.

The next two hours were sheer hell. I remember Megan and Randi quickly losing interest in anything I had to say as I went repeatedly to the bar. I watched, nauseated, as my ex-girlfriend and her date kissed on the patio (which was actually more like a small dog kennel), while I slumped against the wall in an alcove. In fact, when I got tired of slumping, I simply slumped all the way to the floor, as if in a stupor. Shortly thereafter my ex-girlfriend's roommate, who was actually an old friend of mine, tried to persuade me that it wasn't the end of the world and that I should possibly consider standing up.

When I finally did, I decided it was very much past the time to leave. I found Megan with some difficulty, and although she might have guessed I was upset, she did her best to make sure that I knew it didn't make any difference to her. In fact, she and Randi were far more intent on staying and continuing to chat with another woman. When I told them it was time to go home, the third woman took offense and assaulted me with a vulgar monologue that graphically illustrated why women are just like men in terms of bodily functions. Say what? I suggested to Megan and Randi that they either go off to the bathroom to research this information further or take a ride home with me right now. They decided to follow me out to my car.

On the way out of the parking lot, I drove past my ex-girlfriend, who was indecorously leaning against a car and being exceedingly amorous with her new male friend. I lingered on that depressing image as it grew smaller and smaller in my rearview mirror.

After dropping off Randi, I took Megan home. When I expressed an interest in another date, she simply said, "Why?"

Minks and Sables

RICHARD TORRENCE
Richard splits his time between New York City and St. Petersburg, Russia. In St. Petersburg he is both an adviser to the governor and an owner and operator of restaurants.

 I had a secretary who was twenty-six when her forty-five-year-old husband decided that he wanted a younger wife. So he went off after a twenty-two-year-old girl.

My secretary was so pissed off, she vowed, "Next time, I'm not going to marry for love. I'm going to marry for money!" She was determined to do this. So whenever she would meet people, she would try to figure out if they had money.

One day she told me about meeting this guy. "What do you do?" she asked him. "I'm a psychiatrist," he replied. She thought, "Oooooh, he's got some money!"

He invited her out to dinner on a Thursday night. During the meal she said, "Sooooo, you are a psychiatrist?"

He said casually, "Yes. I work for the Public Health Service."

She thought, "Nooooo. Nooooo money!"

Toward the end of the evening, he took her hand and cooed, "What would I have to do to get you into bed?"

"Go into private practice!"

Two months later, he called her up. "Remember me? I've gone into private practice."

"Too late," she quipped, "I just got engaged."

Father Knows Best...?

FRANCINE STACY AND PATRICIA LEVY

Francine is a lawyer in New Jersey.
Patricia works in insurance
in San Diego.

"**W**e can't go out with you tonight," we announced proudly to the boys from our college who were also down in Pompano, Florida for spring break of our sophomore year. "We met these two older men and they're taking us out. They're twenty-five, sexy, rich, well-dressed, intelligent, sweet, and they own an auto business." The guys pretended they weren't impressed and asked us where we met our dates. "My father introduced us."

My dad had never fixed me up before and never did it again. But that day it just happened. He and his friend were having a barbecue lunch with Patricia and me. Two of his friend's buddies stopped by for a visit. They were both really good looking. Ricky was Spanish and had brown hair and brown eyes. Rodney was close to six feet, had blonde hair and green eyes, and was very tan. So, when my father said, "You two ought to take my daughter and her friend out tonight," we were both delighted.

The four of us drove off to this bar in town. We were just hanging out. Nobody was supposed to be with anybody. But things evolved so that I was with Rodney and Patricia was with Ricky. We danced with them and listened to their stories. Ricky told Patricia his father was a senator, that he'd had wonderful jobs and traveled all over the world. Rodney told me about their auto business and his interest in boats. Then Rodney asked the band to dedicate a song to me. I was charmed.

After the dancing, they decided they wanted to show us their place. It all seemed innocent enough. We didn't even question their motives. The place was a modest one-bedroom but the decor indicated the owner had money.

On the way over, for some reason they started using this weird language they had created. It sounded something like Pig Latin, only stranger. It was the one thing about them I disliked.

About 12:30, the four of us were all watching television in the living room. There was a knock on the door and this fat, disheveled, fifty-year-old hippie-type woman barged in with her thirteen-year-old daughter in tow. "You're back on drugs again," she shouted at Ricky, "You've lost your job. I can't believe it!" According to her, this was Ricky's apartment, and he was letting Rodney live there rent-free because Rodney was giving Ricky drugs and had complete control over every aspect of Ricky's life.

Patricia and I didn't know what was happening or what to do, so we fled to the kitchen in search of a way out. "Don't bother, there's only the front door," said the world-weary thirteen-year-old daughter who had calmly retreated to the kitchen for a glass of water. She looked as old as us and was twice as composed.

The daughter explained that her mom had known Ricky and Rodney for years, that Rodney's name wasn't Rodney, that he changed it all the time and had over 100 different aliases. "He moves around from place to place," she informed us, "and he's nothing but trouble." Which seemed pretty obvious now that Rodney was cursing violently at her mother as he tried to force her out of the apartment. The girl said her mom was a social worker who had helped place Ricky in a drug rehab program.

"Ricky, is it because you're a homosexual? Is that why things are so bad for you? Why can't you just deal with it?" we heard the mother scream over the din.

"Yeah, I know I'm gay," Ricky replied, "but I love Rodney and I'm not gonna kick him out."

Patricia and I couldn't believe our ears. We were on a date with two homosexual drug addicts! We were just two little stupid college sophomores who believed we were doomed.

Rodney grew increasingly menacing until finally he roared, "If you don't get out right now, you'll be sorry." With that the woman grabbed her daughter by the arm and proclaimed defiantly, "I'll be back," and walked out.

Patricia and I were still in the kitchen cowering when Rodney entered and tried to make peace. I was totally grossed out by his phoniness. "I didn't know Ricky was gay," Rodney said softly.

"You live with this man in a one-bedroom apartment, and you don't know he's gay?" I snapped back. Once again he insisted that he didn't know. I said, "Listen Rodney, just take us home." In response, Rodney turned cold and he and Ricky started conversing again in their secret language.

On the way back to my father's house, they took a very circuitous route through an unfamiliar, deplorable, drug-infested area. Then, without warning, they pulled into a dark alley and stopped the car. "Listen," Rodney said in a threatening tone, "We've been paying for you all night. We need twenty-five dollars from each of you, now!" We sat there for a moment, unsure what to do. "If you don't give us the money, you're gonna have to get out and walk home." We looked outside the car. Junkies and other scary types were loitering nearby. We didn't know how the hell to get home from there. It was clear they weren't fooling around and that Rodney was capable of violence. We both had the money on us because we'd brought cash for spring break, yet we were still a little reluctant. Then Rodney started yelling at us and we quickly gave them the money and burst into tears. We were sure they'd keep the cash and leave us there anyway.

Then a guy appeared out of the shadows and tapped on the window. They passed him the money. He passed them a white rock. Patricia and I had no clue what it was. We found out later that it was crack cocaine, but since we didn't have anything to do with drugs, we were completely naïve.

They cut a hole in a beer can, put the crack in it, and lit it up like it was a pipe. They inhaled the fumes through the top of the beer can and blew it out into each other's faces. As they exhaled, they were so close, their lips were touching. They didn't want to waste any precious smoke.

Next, they stopped off at a liquor store to buy some more beer. By chance, the police pulled up at the same moment, saw the beer can pipes scattered throughout the car and the two, petrified, nineteen-year-old girls sobbing in the back seat. They arrested Rodney and Ricky.

That evening will haunt us forever. Since then, we've been very selective about our dates, as well as those who fix us up.

Dressed to Kill

LINDA CHEN

*Born and raised in Boston, Linda
lives in Los Angeles, where she shoots
production still photographs for films
and celebrity lifestyle pieces for
magazines worldwide. She's still single
and looking for Mr. Right.*

"**W**hat are you looking for tonight?" my girl-friend inquired as we surveyed the single men below us from the Art Deco balcony. Everybody at this poolside cocktail party had graduated from an Ivy League college. "A Caucasian version of my father," I joked. "But a little more adventurous."

"What does that mean?" she mocked.

"Staid, serene, and East Coast-educated. A guy who likes to read and play bridge and doesn't like to sweat. You know, Chinese people don't like to sweat."

Then Chuck appeared over my shoulder and I thought my wish had come true. He seemed smooth and pulled together. He wore a charcoal Brooks Brothers suit and an over-the-ear haircut. He was twenty-six, energetic, a second-year associate at a major law firm, and the proud owner of a new house in West Los Angeles.

Over cocktails I told him I was a girl who was into anything. He responded with witty innuendo and took my number. When he called, he asked if it was okay for us to go out on Saturday afternoon instead of the evening. I said it was fine. "Dress casually," he instructed me.

Saturday afternoon, a scrawny guy with spindly legs and jeans knocked on my door. (Padded shoulders and good tailoring did wonders for this guy!) As we climbed into his convertible sports car he informed me that we had to make a quick stop at his new house on the way.

The house was in complete disarray. Boxes everywhere, no furniture, and no completed bathrooms. I wondered how a well-groomed guy could live in a place that had no running water. He claimed he took showers at the gym and liked the idea of roughing it.

To my amazement, Chuck started pawing through bubble wrap and pulled out two rifles, several pistols, holsters, and assorted boxes of ammo in different shapes and colors. Apparently skeet and trap shooting were Chuck's bimonthly ritual; his chance to get outdoors and socialize with the boys. The closest I'd ever come to a gun before was riflery class at camp when I was eight. But I was willing to give the sport a try. This made Chuck buoyant and optimistic.

His enthusiasm manifested itself on the freeway as we drove out of town through the desert. Top down, Chuck gunned his convertible to ninety miles per hour. I clung to the door handle, fearing for my life and my contact lenses. Not eager to be a nag, I politely mentioned that he was exceeding the speed limit. I figured that recognition of unlawful behavior would mean something to an attorney. He reduced his speed to eighty-seven and cackled madly, boasting about the dozens of speeding tickets he had yet to pay. Right then I knew I could never trust him to drive my future children to piano lessons. I dreaded what would happen when he held a gun.

The firing range was a vast sandpit behind a dilapidated coffee shop in the middle of nowhere. Six huge, barrel-chested rednecks with callused hands lined up to pay for their turn at the skeet shooting range. I waited behind them with my soft-handed Ivy Leaguer. Everyone seemed to be aware of the fact that I was the only woman (or Asian) in the joint. I felt like an infiltrator, an outcast. Chuck started to chew and spit tobacco, just like the boys. I opted against full assimilation.

Donning earplugs, I valiantly took my position at the skeet shooting pit in front of the unfriendly crowd. The attendant checked me out and gave me all the necessary safety precautions. Chuck began coaching from the sidelines. The object of this game, I learned, is to blast the clay pigeons midair as they "fly" on a diagonal axis from one pigeon house to the other. Easy enough, I thought. Rifle flailing, I blasted away. I missed. And missed. At almost every target point, I missed. Chuck swaggered into the pit and took his turn with the gun. He was nearly as inept as I was but he still lorded his success over me.

We then moved over to the trap shooting range. The object of this game is to blast the clay discus midair as it is propelled in an outward trajectory from the trap house to the distant horizon. As fate would have it, I was good at this. Very good. So good the rednecks stopped to watch and applaud in amazement. They marveled even more when they heard it was my first time. Chuck was jealous and discouraged. In contrast, the musclemen were enthusiastic and supportive. In sheer delight, one of the towering bruisers lent me his rifle filled with magnum loads. I blasted away, annihilating the trap targets. Others handed me their guns. I smashed more pigeons to smithereens.

I could feel brain tissue jostling violently inside my head. My shoulder, the one supporting the rifle, felt dislocated. I needed a bottle of aspirin desperately! But I had gotten into the rhythm of the sport, and despite the pain, I was euphoric. I had discovered an enormous talent I had no idea I possessed and no interest in pursuing further. It was pure glee.

Chuck was crushed. On the way home, he gunned the motor to 100 miles per hour. This time I didn't object. The Ivy League Outlaw had proven himself to be more deadly on the freeway than on the firing range. And I was anxious to get home.

As he pulled out of my driveway, I checked to see if he'd left any rubber.

Hot Cars and Sticky Fingers

SHARON CORBETT

Sharon is a supervisor of a telephone room in Denver.

Ted was twenty-four and ugly, but at nineteen I was attracted to him because I always liked nice cars and he always seemed to have a nice car. He also had this natural talent for auto body painting that I wished I had. He could take a piece of crap car and make it look just gorgeous in a couple of hours. It was awesome.

Ted and I had met each other three years earlier while out cruising, which was the thing to do in Denver back in the '70s. My best friend and I were driving down the main drag in my classic, red-and-white '55 Ford, looking good, when Ted and his buddy pulled up alongside us and asked if we wanted a ride. I wound up tooling around with Ted in his beautiful, blue Corvette while my girlfriend cruised with his friend in a Cougar. It didn't work out between my friend and his buddy, but Ted and I became friends.

Two, three in the morning, we'd see each other on the street. Go get hotdogs. Sit and talk for an hour. He was so worldly. Then he'd go home alone and I'd go home alone.

When I was nineteen, however, Ted finally took me on an actual date. He picked me up in another hot Corvette, a 1976 show car called Kaleidoscope that had won a trophy at World of Wheels in Denver. It had this pearl white body with a thousand different colored ribbons painted all over it and was just so impressive.

After we had dinner, Ted and I started cruising along the main street. We went around the block, drove down a couple of miles, turned around, and looped back. It seemed like we were staying in the same area, but since Ted was so charismatic and entertaining, I just didn't notice. All of sudden he said to me, "Would you like to drive the Vet?" I'd never driven a show car before and geez, I was delighted.

After we switched places, Ted said, "I want you to pull over to the side of the curb."

"Well why?"

"Wouldn't you like to get the feel of the car with nobody in it? What we'll do is, you stop and let me out here, go on around the block, come back and meet me at the opposite end of this block, okay?"

I did just that. When I returned, Ted was waving and moving towards the car with his coat tossed over one arm. I hadn't even pulled up to the curb before he took two leaps into the street, ripped open the passenger door, jumped into the car and produced four, large, expensive, wire hubcaps from under his coat. "Step on it," he commanded.

"Excuse me?"

"Drive, drive." He jammed two of the hubcaps between the seats and the other two on the floor in front.

"What's going on, Ted?" He just ignored me. I drove down probably a mile. By then, I'd gotten the shakes. This made Ted angry. "Shari, you're gonna get us stopped by a cop. Pull over."

We pulled over and I hesitated. I was scared that when we switched places, Ted would try to leave me there and drive off. So, as soon as I heard the engine, I jumped back in the car. "Ted, did you steal these hubcaps?"

He smiled casually. "Now why would a guy like me do a thing like that?"

"I don't know? You're the one with the hubcaps."

"Nah," Ted said nonchalantly. "That was a friend's car and I knew how pissed off he'd be if I took his hubcaps." He was so convincing in his claim that it was a prank that it seemed stupid for me to say anything more.

A couple weeks later some friends confirmed my hunch about Ted. They said he had a good sideline business stealing hubcaps, radios, leather steering wheels, and anything else that could be easily lifted from a car. He'd even take orders. I guess he must have had an order for hubcaps the night of our date and when he saw them, he went for them, because he knew from experience, no car's going to stay parked in the same spot forever.

I had intended to report him to the police until I realized the man knows where I live. If he could steal hubcaps, he could certainly steal my entire red-and-white classic '55 Ford. I wasn't looking for that kind of retribution.

Bible Class Bamboozle

ED WISE

A former pipe fitter, Ed works maintenance for a paper mill and is studying for his engineering degree at Old Dominion College in Virginia Beach, Virginia. He's now married.

When I was twenty-four, I wasn't interested in hot cars and fast women. I was interested in helping elderly people at the church, working with kids and the mentally handicapped, and attending my adult bible class. Most of the people in bible class knew I did not appreciate blind dates. But when this new woman joined up, I began to hear some casual talk about my marital status. Mind you, I'm not a movie star, but I'm not bad looking. I have a good build and I exercise. At twenty-four, I'd never been married and didn't have any kids. So from the perspective of a matchmaker, I was a pretty good prospect.

I called the "perfect girl" a lady from Bible class recommended. She sounded pleasant, asked me a few particulars about myself, and then started right in telling me about her national marketing business. I told her I thought it'd be neat to own a business. "Well how'd you like to see my business?" she asked enthusiastically.

The question caught me off guard. "Sure, I'd love to see it sometime."

"Good, let's get together Thursday and I'll show it to you."

I told her that normally I didn't go out on weeknights, except to teach Sunday school, because I had to get up at 4:30 in the morning for my pipe-fitting job. She said she wouldn't be able to do anything on the weekend so I agreed to accommodate her schedule.

I asked her how I should dress. She said casually, so I was pretty surprised when she showed up all decked out in high heels, make-up, cologne, an attractive green dress, and a big smile. When I offered to go in and change she said, "No, we don't have time." I thought, "Why in the world don't we have time? Does her store close early or something?"

Before I could say anything she said, "Let's go eat fast food." I'm not a fan of fast food and had planned to take her to a decent restaurant. In fact I told her, "If I had suggested a fast food place, you would have thought I was a cheapskate." The comment passed right by her because she was dead set on McDonald's. She was also dead set on doing the driving. Although it made me uncomfortable having her control the whole date, I didn't want to make a fuss.

At McDonald's, I tried to get specific about what she actually sold in her national marketing business. She said, "Oh we do this and that, just little things." I didn't get the impression she was interested in me, as much as she was interested in me not asking her many questions.

After the meal, she drove us down to the shopping mall, which is a good twenty miles from my house. I assumed she owned a store inside the mall. That seemed exciting. We went upstairs, and she led me into this conference room that was full of eighty people in fancy suits and ties. They were all real happy to meet me and stuffed business cards in my pocket as they shook hands and flashed their teeth like salesmen. No wonder. She'd hornswoggled me to an Amway convention!

Some people would have stomped out and rented a cab right then, but that's not my nature. "How late does this thing last?" I asked. She assured me it lasted about an hour. This was at seven in the evening.

For the next three-and-a-half hours the leader talked nonstop hypocrisy. He talked about God and how great God was. The next minute he was swearing and hawking the Amway products that made him a million bucks—cars, soap powders, and lingerie that looked like it came from that place out in California called Fredericks of Hollywood. Then he jumped back to God and told the enthralled crowd to scour the church for new prospects. "You know what we're looking for—people who think right and look good and could make a good company impression." Evidently I was an easy prospect.

At 10:30 p.m. the leader declared, "Well, we're half way through now." I was so upset, I pulled her aside, "You know I have to get up at 4:30. Take me home, now!"

On the way out my date didn't even apologize. "Well, what did you think?" she asked.

I was furious. "I thought we were going on a date. I thought we'd become friends. If I had known you wanted to sell me something, I wouldn't have come."

She tried to worm out of it. "Well, I thought you just wanted to know about my business." Sure.

As she dropped me off she hinted around about wanting to get together again. I said probably not. Unlike her, I prefer to be honest.

A few months later I heard that she had joined a Baptist church that had twelve hundred people in attendance every Sunday. I thought, "Well, that'll just be perfect. There she'll find herself a lot of good prospects for a lot of bad dates."

A Rose by Any Other Name Is Not as Sweet

ANNETTE BONET

Annette Bonet is an advertising copywriter who lives in Chicago.

I was twenty-eight and between jobs and looking at the ads online, when, just for fun, I checked out the personals. To my surprise, I found one with substance. Tom was a thirty-nine-year-old, divorced CEO of a small manufacturing company and a graduate of University of Chicago. Besides that, he had just gotten his private investigator's license and was developing that business on the side. He also taught aerobics two nights a week. I sent him an e-mail and he responded right away with an attractive picture of him and his little boy. He had this intense personality and was very intellectual and very romantic.

After talking back and forth for two weeks, both online and on the phone, we decided to meet for dinner. The evening went so well, we ended up seeing each other almost every day after that.

By the third day of dating, he told me that he loved me and that I was his soulmate. I didn't want to say "I love you" back, although I did have strong feelings. Still, there was something not quite right about him. For instance, things kept slipping out, like he had three children, not one, and he was CEO of his father's company, not his own. But I brushed off those inconsistencies because otherwise things were really great.

About two weeks into the relationship, instant messages started popping up on my computer screen while I was online job searching. They were from five or six eligible men—doctors, business owners, etc.—asking me to have coffee and sending me their pictures. Since I was new to America Online and hadn't been approached like that before, I didn't know how these people got my name. But I looked up each of their profiles in the member directory and then wrote back, "You sound like a nice man, but I'm seeing someone."

After a week in which several more men hit on me, I got the intuitive feeling that Tom was checking to see if I was flirting online by using fake screen names (which made sense given his private investigator sideline). So, I grabbed the cordless phone and called Tom while I was online talking to one of the other guys. In the meantime, I started asking very open-ended questions of my online buddy. The dialogue on the screen just stopped. At that point I asked Tom directly if he was sending me instant messages. He said no; there was a power outage and his computer just crashed.

Then I started getting smart. I wrote down the names of all the men who IM'd me and once again looked up their profiles. Most were no longer listed in the member directory. Now I was sure something was up. I confronted Tom with my hunch. He denied it. I became uncomfortable and pulled back a bit, which made Tom more suspicious—which made no sense to me since I was spending almost every night with him.

My next clue came when I was over at his house checking my e-mail on his computer. I noticed Tom's "buddy list" in the corner of the screen said two of his sixty buddies were online at that time. Sixty buddies? How did he find so many?

I went home, looked up Tom's profile again and discovered that he'd added a web page to his profile. I clicked on it and found three full pages about who he was and what he was looking for in a woman. I couldn't believe it. He was still searching for girls while he was telling me he wanted to marry me and have children. No wonder he thought I was cheating.

The next time I was at his house, checking my e-mail on his computer, I opened his files for two seconds while he wasn't looking. In there I found eight hundred photos of women. I also spotted a file called Tahiti. Bingo! One of the men who asked me out online sent me a photo of him taken in Tahiti. Now I was sure he was using fake names.

But I still couldn't let on. Instead, although I felt guilty, I decided to catch him in the act.

I went home, logged on and made up a fake screen name and a very basic profile that wasn't at all enticing, and sent him a note. "Hi my name is Cathy. I'm studying at Northwestern Medical School. I liked your web page. If you're not seeing anyone, please let me know." Two hours later, he e-mailed Cathy a three page letter. "Hi Cathy. So refreshing to hear from you. You sound so intelligent. Blah, blah, blah." He even put in the same quotes he sent me when we first talked. I got sick to my stomach.

Later that day, I logged on again. As soon as I did, he sent an instant message to Cathy. "So, Cathy, you're studying at Northwestern Medical School. Well, I'm studying to get my Ph.D.," which was a total lie. I typed back as Cathy, "Are you involved with anyone? Because I once had a bad experience and I want to make sure you're not coming out of divorce or dating anyone else." He typed back, "No. Your timing is perfect. I just broke up with someone a week ago." My stomach turned again and I typed back "F*** YOU, Tom. This is Annette."

Two seconds later the phone started ringing. "Annette, you don't understand. Online doesn't mean anything to me. It's just something fun for me to do," he said crying.

I replied, "Don't ever call me again," and I hung up the phone.

That didn't stop him. He drove over to my house and kept calling from downstairs until I let him come up. I wanted to hear his explanation, get the closure, and move on. This time he got even more dramatic and teary. "Here, I'll prove online means nothing. I'll throw my computer out the window. Or better yet, I'll give you my passcodes for my cell phone and my computer." And he proceeded to rattle off the information. I told him I still felt uncomfortable and sent him home.

As soon as he left, I signed onto the computer as him, and after a lot of mistakes, I called up his billing records. It turns out he had *thirty different screen names* he used to stalk me at all hours of the day and night. Later, in a therapy session he dragged me to by convincing me it would help him solve his problem with trust, I learned that he'd been in contact with 350 women over the past two years. But he insisted that I was very special to him and he desperately wanted things to work out with us. I thought to myself, "If he stalked even a dozen or two of those 350 women with thirty screen names like he did me, how could he have time to do anything else?" This guy lives online and he's nuts.

I left the therapy session and told Tom I couldn't see him anymore. He kept e-mailing me, begging me to give him another chance. But three days after therapy, his ad was back up online, as was his web page. So much for soul mates.

Talk Is Cheap

FRANK MOFFET
*Frank is a producer of film and TV
shows based in New York.*

When I was twenty-six years old and teaching school, I got an opportunity to work as a production assistant on the set of a low-budget movie that was being made in the town where I grew up, on the shore north of Boston. It was a cheap horror film which became best known for playing as the second feature of a double-bill at drive-ins around the south.

Among the cast members was an extraordinarily beautiful actress named Elinore Crawford. She was a thirty-three-year-old Jean Harlow look-alike—tall with platinum blonde hair and a fantastic figure. On the set I was transfixed by her. In the small town where I lived, I'd never seen anyone like this before.

We talked a lot between takes. I was always very polite and attentive to her needs, as I was to everybody in the cast and crew. My mother and father had trained me until it was second nature to say "yes, ma'am" and "yes, sir." I also wanted to make a good impression and change careers.

Soon, I learned from one of the other people on the picture that Elinore thought I was nice and I should ask her out. I was quite surprised. There were a lot of handsome, muscular guys around who, at first blush, would have seemed more her type. I invited her to supper and made a Saturday night reservation at the best restaurant in town—a classic seaside resort fish restaurant with a great view of the harbor.

I put on my basic outfit in those days, which was a pair of chinos and a blue blazer; got into my pick-up truck, which could only be started by shoving a screwdriver between the connection and the battery; and drove to her hotel. She emerged from the lobby wearing a silver sable jacket; low-cut, tight, ice blue pants; and silver spike-heeled shoes. Under the coat was a skin-tight, button-up blouse that you could see her nipples right through. She was an amazing piece of work. And when she strutted into the big, wooden dining room of the restaurant, the entire, solidly middle-class crowd of local bankers, doctors, business-men, and their wives, couldn't help but stare. It was obvious that Elinore was from another world.

We talked a lot over dinner. I listened to what she had to say for quite a period of time. She was an orphan from Ireland who had come over to America and had become successful. I had a certain sense that she didn't earn her living only by acting, but I was too polite to press for details.

About midway through the meal, I asked quite sincerely, "Why did you like me?"

She replied, "Well you said 'ma'am' and you listened." At that moment, I realized I had been chosen. She was going to grace me with her favors.

So, we went back to her hotel for a blissful evening. Besides having an incredible body—which she adorned with fancy, translucent underwear—and liquid moves, she was the most amazing dirty talker I've ever heard. She was very specific about what she liked and how to do it. I was happy to oblige. Later, she announced it was my turn and then she really kicked into gear.

As she worked on me, she gave me a verbal preview of whatever she was about to do. Then, just as I'd gotten all hot thinking about it, she'd execute the move with complete finesse and start all over again with something else to titillate me. She had a real rhythm going. It was phenomenal.

The next day was Sunday, and since we were having such a lovely time, I invited her over to my parents' house for the afternoon. My mother and father were away on a cruise and I was house-sitting while they were gone. My parents lived on a cliff with a little cove and an island in front of it.

As soon as Elinore saw the house, she wanted me to photograph her on the rocks. We climbed down the cliff. She stripped off all her clothes and paraded around. I took some great shots. She put her outfit back on—which once again consisted of tight slacks, spiked heels and another see-through blouse—and returned to the house.

She was wandering around the living room waiting for me to fix some snacks, when my parents suddenly walked in the door. Thank God they didn't show up five minutes earlier because the sight of her naked body would have given my dad a premature heart attack.

My father, a southern gentleman of the first order, almost fell over himself as he offered her drinks. He was the most charming and polite I'd ever seen him. My mother reacted slightly differently. Before the afternoon was over, she asked me to step into another room and hissed, "What is that?"

I said lightly, "Oh mother, that's an actress."

She retorted with a sneer, "That's no actress." A year later, I learned that was probably true.

One day, I was in New Haven visiting a friend. With nothing better to do on a rainy afternoon, we stopped by the local porno movie theater. Much to my surprise, who showed up halfway through the film but my pal Elinore, performing salacious acts on a lucky fellow. Yet what was ultimately distressing to me was what I'd thought was the most extraordinary, intimate, provocative dirty talk I'd ever heard in my life was being spoken on the screen, almost verbatim, to her "acting" partner.

My friend thought I was a hero. But the real hero was my clairvoyant mother.

Faint of Heart

NICOLE DILLENBERG
*Nicole is a published poet and an
underground actress who has appeared
in independent films. She abridges
audiobook manuscripts for publishing
houses and writes screenplays.*

It was the dinner party of my life. I'd been in love
with this boy since childhood and had moved back
to England just to find him again. It took some
doing, but two months after moving into a flat, I
managed to track him down. My best friend at the
time was house-sitting for a photographer, so we
decided to use her place to throw a dinner party
for eight, at which the object of my affections and
I could be reunited in a non-threatening manner.

During our school years together, I hadn't
understood my crush's social standing. It was only
upon my return to England that I was bombarded
with this new information. As a result, I was feeling rather intimidated by upper-class English social
mores (and my awareness of them) as I arrived at
the photographer's house that night. I should have
taken it as a bad omen when I crossed the thresh-
old and saw the society photographs covering the

walls, many of which were portraits of my lost love's relatives. Horrified, my best friend and I took down all the photos the gauche social-climbing photographer had on display and hid them under the bed. We then, of course, had the problem of the nails sticking out of every wall so we started hanging coasters and potholders and things at random, whatever we could find, to cover the blank spots.

I was stirring the broad beans when I heard the doorbell. All the other guests had already arrived so I knew it was *him*. I made my friend go to the door. I was fully prepared for this boy to have become a geek and thought myself particularly mature to have realized that I might find myself disappointed.

When he finally stepped from the darkened hallway into the room it was like a bolt of lightning hit me. I'd never been so attracted to anyone in my life and without even thinking about decorum, I threw myself into his arms.

The next thing I remember, all seven people in the room were dead silent. I was still hugging my beloved, but his arms were at his sides. Apparently, I was so nervous I had blacked out. I have no idea how long we stood there—two seconds, ten minutes? All I know is I was so embarrassed that I hid in the kitchen for the rest of the evening. Later, when I asked my best friend what happened, she was so English about it she wouldn't even talk. I never would have dreamed of grilling our guests about the debacle. They wouldn't have said anything anyway; they were even more English than my friend.

To this day, on the rare occasions when I see the boy who (quite literally) took my breath away, he steers clear. Thank God we didn't kiss that night. Who knows what might have happened?

Mountains Out of Molehills

SYLVIA FRANKS
*Based in Nashville and Los Angeles,
Sylvia works as a production
accountant on films and TV shows.
She's still single and having bad dates.*

Before I went on my date with the successful owner of a couple of record stores in Nashville, my girlfriend told me that I had to kiss him goodnight. "It doesn't matter how much of a prude you are. He's cute and he has money, he'll expect it." I agreed with her and thought that at nineteen I should change my ways.

I had met my date the night before at the Smuggler's Inn, a place in Nashville were everybody hung out in 1976. A bunch of us girls would go there two or three times a week after work and dance on the tiny dance floor next to the bar.

While I was dancing, I noticed this man watching me, but he never asked me to dance. He just came over and introduced himself, complimented me, and asked for my number at work. Since he was very well mannered and attractive, I gave it to him.

The next night he picked me up in a vintage Jaguar that was so low it almost sat on the ground.

During the bumpy ride to the restaurant, he mentioned that he liked to bring this car on his dates. I thought it was his way of saying it was impressive to women.

Over dinner he asked me if I knew what had attracted him to me on the dance floor. I had no idea. "Your breasts," he said simply. If you have long blonde hair, blue eyes, and weigh 100 pounds soaking wet, you think that's what attracts men, not your totally flat chest!

On the way back home, I stared out the window in silence wondering how I could have been such a poor judge of character. When I finally looked back over at my date, I found him staring intently at my breasts, as they shook under my little, black shell top. He smiled and said calmly, "As you can see, the reason I like to bring this car on dates is, well, it's real bumpy." Suddenly I had real sympathy for what girls with big breasts go through!

I kept hearing my girlfriend's words of caution as he walked me to the front door and decided I'd have to let him give me a smack kiss goodnight. But just as we made lip contact, he grabbed the bottom of my shirt, threw it back over my head and started to study my bare breasts (I wasn't wearing a bra) like it was a normal part of a date! Enraged and scared, I jerked the shirt back down and banged on the front door. He was in no hurry to leave. He didn't feel like he'd violated me. He just strolled to his car and drove off very slowly, leaving me in a panicked state.

I didn't hear anything from him until a couple of weeks later when he called up and told me he had tickets and backstage passes for the Fleetwood Mac "Rumors" concert. I really wanted to go, but I was still furious. "I can't believe you have the nerve to call me after what you did to me. You haven't called, you haven't apologized—" He acted like I was making a big deal out of nothing.

The next morning I went out to my car and sitting on top of it were three things: a big carton of record albums, a box of itty, bitty baby Band-Aids, and a note that said, "You really made a mountain out of a molehill, I mean, two molehills."

Mr. Big Shot

MIKHAL ZAMBON
Mikhal ran an alternative nightclub before changing careers. She is now a designer of creative flooring surfaces. She lives in Las Vegas.

The lifeguard from Australia said he came here to explore America, so I volunteered to show him the sights. It wasn't much of a sacrifice. He was blonde-blue-eyed-gorgeous, well built, and happened to be free on Saturday night.

Since he didn't have a car, I drove by way of Sunset Boulevard out to Malibu beach. I'd made reservations at Gladstones, an oceanfront restaurant frequented by families, tourists, and couples.

We hadn't talked much at happy hour the night before when we'd met, so I asked him what he wanted to do now that he was here. "I plan to join Gold's Gym," he replied quite naturally. Gold's Gym is a mecca for Los Angeles body builders.

"That's all you want to do?" I asked incredulously. He was only twenty-four years old. "What do you really want to do?"

"I want to be a big man," he grunted.

"Well, that's ambition for you!" I thought. But I was willing to overlook his shortcomings for a while longer because he was so cute and the night was young.

On the way back to the car, we were inspired to go for a moonlit stroll on the beach. In my flat shoes, I followed him as he climbed down the craggy ridge. He took a seat right away on a rock. I continued to walk around. I could have sworn I heard rats and wanted to be sure I wouldn't destroy the mood by sitting down on one. Moments later, some people shouted at us from a distance. I glanced back at my date and realized why. He was getting his rocks off on the rocks. Maybe that's what he meant by "being a big man."

Fire Down Below

TIMOTHY SMITH
*Timothy is a Vice President with
Preferred Payment Systems, a
healthcare cost-containment company.
He lives in Pennsylvania with his
wife and three children.*

I pretty much thought I was immune to poison ivy when I somehow developed a horrible case after doing some outdoor work in short shorts. Everything was swollen and itchy from my calves to my waist, including my genitals, which were the sorest of all. Under normal conditions, I would have nursed my bad luck in private with the help of cortisone cream. Unfortunately, I had set up a date three weeks earlier with a tall, twenty-four-year-old, gorgeous brunette who looked like a model, and there was no way I was going to beg off. The only solution, I decided, was to put on a pair of baggy linen pants with a drawstring waist and no underwear and just go for it.

I arrived at my date's house and was just getting acquainted with her parents, when a vision in white descended the stairs with a beautiful Irish Setter in tow. The dog bounded across the room, jumped up, and wrapped his paws around me like I was an old family friend. I pushed his paws down, and as I did, one paw caught the drawstring and snapped it, while the other paw snagged my pants and pulled them right down to my ankles.

"Oh my God, what is that?!" my date's mortified mother cried out as she stared at a body that undoubtedly looked like it had contracted a terminal case of the chicken pox. Her father chortled. Mom shot him a dirty look. My date was so embarrassed, she gawked and blushed in stunned silence.

"Well, I guess we should be going," I said as I pulled up my trousers. "I have reservations at the London Chop House." What else could I do?

The London Chop House was a well-known, expensive steak-and-ale place that attracted people on expense accounts. The maître d' seated us at a middle table in a full room off the main dining room. Things were moving along. The incident proved to be a good icebreaker. We laughed over snail appetizers and red wine. Then, when I reached for the bread rolls, I accidentally knocked my date's glass of red wine all over her beautiful, white, silk dress. She jumped up trying to shake off the stain. I jumped up, trying to blot it with a napkin. But at that exact moment, the safety pin that her parents had provided to hold up my pants decided to unsnap and impale my already tender organ. "Oooohhh!" I howled involuntarily and grabbed at my crotch, right in the middle of this very discreet, high-class restaurant. "Who brought these two people in?" sniffed one snooty customer. The others just turned and glared.

Not surprisingly, our appetites disappeared instantly. I flagged the waiter and handed him my credit card. "We don't take plastic," he sneered loudly. "Only cash." Once again all eyes turned to me. I squirmed and looked at my feet. My date pulled out her purse and paid for dinner, literally adding insult to injury.

Underwear Makes the Man

RACHAEL KLEIN
*Rachael is a sales consultant
who lives in Santa Fe.*

I had been with my husband a really long time, so when we finally got married, we wanted a change. We quit our jobs, borrowed some money, moved to Colorado, and started a business. We worked like dogs for three years and made a ton of money, but we had no social life outside of each other.

Then the business started going bad through my husband's mismanagement, and he started spending all of his time at the office. I felt lonely and bored and neglected until I discovered the Internet. Right away it became my surrogate social life. I'd spend my evenings online talking to people in other places. Next I became more adventurous and went into different chat rooms, like the Millionaires' Lounge or this dominant/submissive location called the Dungeon. I'd watch the chats scroll by. It was fascinating. From there, I discovered cyber sex and once I did that, I became addicted. Majorly addicted.

One night I met this guy in a chat room and we clicked, which is very easy to do online because you're not with the person, so you're filling in the blanks with your own picture of what you want them to be. He was married and lived in Texas. That was fine by me. I figured it would be safe.

From that day on, the Texan and I had this passionate, online affair that was "the best sex I never had." All the while I kept thinking, "nothing is going to happen. This is just a hobby for me. My husband doesn't care about my needs. He's an alcoholic and only cares about his business."

Then, despite my guilt, I took a bold step. I rented a secret post office box. The Texan sent me a card with a picture of him, and after that, I received letters from him every day for two months. Incredible, long love letters. In addition to that, he would call me on my cell phone in my car every day at lunchtime when I was working. The affair got so intense, we'd say things like, "I don't care if you have four eyes and weigh five hundred pounds, I love you."

Finally my resistance wore down. I was married, so I didn't want to sleep with him, but I just had to meet this man for lunch. Since the Texan traveled a lot for business, we made a plan to meet in San Diego where my mother lived.

I flew to San Diego, rented a car, drove to my mother's house, and changed into a sexy suit. He was waiting for me at his hotel. I got back in my car and started driving, but I was so nervous, I took half a Valium and still had to stop every three blocks to calm myself down.

When I reached the hotel, he climbed into my car, and after all that romantic build up and all that talking, we couldn't even speak to each other. We could only stare. We went to dinner. I couldn't eat. I couldn't function. I was so jumpy and guilty and confused.

After dinner, we returned to his hotel room. We started to mess around and as he took off his clothes, I noticed he was wearing strange long-john-like underwear. I asked him why and he told me it was the special underwear that Mormons wear. This guy wasn't just your average Mormon, he held an official position in the Mormon church! I couldn't believe it. In all his letters, he'd left out the one detail that governed every aspect of his life, down to what he was prepared to do with me that night in the hotel room. According to him, as a Mormon, he could do everything with me except have intercourse because only intercourse was cheating. I was dying to know what tenet of the Mormon church said that, but I didn't bother asking. The rest of the weekend was going so well, and I assumed this was a one shot transgression for me.

I went back to Boulder, and being the idiot that I am, I told my husband. He flipped out. We went back into therapy. I felt very guilty and yet, I didn't stop communicating with the Mormon who was hotly pursuing me.

Soon, he was so obsessed, he got in his car and drove straight through to Boulder. I met him at a hotel. He'd laid roses on the bed and a teddy bear (both not my style) and was now primed to have intercourse. Once that happened, the whole tone of the relationship changed. Whereas pre-sex he never uttered a cuss word, now he was telling me he wanted to f*** my brains out and sending me pornographic scenarios of things he wanted to do to me and begging me to shave all my pubic hair. Simultaneously, he was sending books on Mormonism and trying to convert me. He even mailed me a tape called "How a Nice Jewish Boy Became a Mormon."

I told him repeatedly, both online and in bed, I'm a non-religious person, I'm Jewish culturally, and if I was going to be religious, I wouldn't choose what I consider to be a crackpot, eighty-year-old religion full of secrecy and sexism and silly undergarments. And what has it done for you? You're lying in bed having an affair with me!

This crazy combination of sex and conversion went on for six months, until one day, when my secretary put a call through to me at my office. It was his wife. She had discovered a letter from me in his briefcase and decided to call me at the office, with my husband working in the next room. I felt so terrible, I actually threw up in the wastebasket.

I picked up the phone and gave one-word answers to this woman who seemed intelligent and nice. Just as we were about to hang up I said, "I know it doesn't matter at this point but I'm sorry." That opened the floodgate and every story about their lives and his cheating came pouring out.

Two hours later I got another call. This one was from whatever is the equivalent to a priest in the Mormon church asking if I wanted to be counseled by him. The man said they were going to have their version of an intervention at church next week, though I shouldn't warn the Texan, and did I have anything to share with him that could be helpful to the process. I just snapped. I said, "Don't call me. I don't see him anymore. My husband knows. We're in therapy. I want nothing to do with you people!"

They ex-communicated him. His wife divorced him. I left my husband. And our relationship fizzled. It seems once we were no longer each other's forbidden fruit, the thrill was gone.

The Big Chill

JANE DOE

*Jane is an educator from Winnipeg,
Manitoba in Canada.*

My parents' house had a white picket fence just like the one I thought I'd have to go along with the little white house, the five children, and the "happily ever after" life I was planning to lead once my first love proposed. When you're a twenty-one-year-old virgin and madly in love, you think it's just a matter of time before that happens.

It was spring. My twenty-one-year-old boyfriend had just finished writing his finals for his engineering degree and we wanted to celebrate. Sunday night we got totally blotto. About three in the morning, we drove back to my parents' house, where I was still living, and parked his car in the backyard without giving it a second thought. One thing led to another and, emboldened by drink, passion got the better of us. We never even had a chance to move to the back seat. Inside, my mother, who could never sleep soundly unless her baby (me) was home, decided she was quite thirsty and wandered down to the kitchen to fetch a glass of water. As she was pouring, she happened to glance out the kitchen window, which faced the backyard. The back door light was on, providing just enough illumination for her to see a bare bum bobbing up and down in the back seat of a car.

The next thing I knew, the car door abruptly swung open and we were assaulted by a powerful spray of icy water! As I pulled up my pants in record time, I surveyed the scene. My devastated family was standing there with my dad holding the chilling garden hose.

Dad screamed. Mom screamed. My boyfriend screamed. I wanted to scream. Instead I muzzled my boyfriend and told him to get the hell out of there.

Mom kept repeating, "You'll be pregnant. You'll be pregnant."

I kept repeating, "We hadn't done anything yet, I couldn't be pregnant!"

My older sister kept repeating, "What's done is done. What's done is done. We may as well just go to bed."

The next morning, I woke up early and was about to head off to teach school without confronting the family, when I discovered a little note: "We did it for your own good, dear. We love you so much." Thanks, Mom. It was just what a traumatized twenty-one-year-old virgin really needed to read.

The dousing undoubtedly put out the flame of my first serious romance. At the same time, it ignited a lifelong passion for making love in the shower.

Two years ago, after a divorce, my first love reappeared and tried to rekindle our relationship. This time it was my turn to pour cold water on his fire.

The Sweet Smell of Love

KATHERINE EDWARDS

*Katherine works as a receptionist for
an ear, nose, and throat doctor
in Los Angeles.*

Despite the fact that he was the kind of guy who usually sniffled, he was considered a good catch in high school. Tall, thin, dark, green eyes, really cute. A popular artsy type. I had my eye on him maybe six months. Finally, after a friend introduced us, he asked me out.

We had dinner at a sandwich place in Westwood. Before we left the restaurant, I freshened up in the bathroom. He put his arm around me when we walked out to his car and gave me a nice hug before we got inside.

On the drive to the movies he started to itch. A few minutes later, red bumps appeared on his skin. They spread everywhere—hands, arms, neck, head. There were more on his face than anywhere else. Most were the size of a dime and very painful. We couldn't figure out what it was. Next he developed a fever which rose so rapidly he was sweating, shaking, and short of breath. Soon, his swelling got so bad, he looked like he had been stung by a swarm of wasps.

We both knew it was serious and decided to go right to the emergency room of the nearest hospital. On the way over he mentioned he was highly allergic to certain things. I wondered if it was something unusual in the car. He suspected it could be my perfume. I'd sprayed it on quite liberally after dinner.

The doctors confirmed it. I felt awful. During the five hours we waited in the emergency room, I apologized repeatedly for the suffering I'd caused him.

After that, the hospital transferred him to a recovery room and sent in a candy striper to check his temperature and pulse. He perked up instantly when she walked in the room. For some reason, the candy striper seemed vaguely familiar to me too. "Oh wow, you work here now?" he asked enthusiastically. "How have you been?" He introduced us and I realized that she was the girlfriend he had broken up with five months before. The two of us were like night and day. I'm tall and thin and quiet. She was short and loud and wild.

My date and his ex kept talking and talking. I kept getting pushed farther and farther into the corner of the room. After about half an hour of watching them, it was so obvious they were thrilled to see each other and were still really in love, I figured I'd do the guy a favor and leave.

The next time I saw them he had his arm around her. They stayed together until we all graduated from high school. As a result, I consider myself their accidental cupid.

Kierkegaard Slept Here

HANNA SIMON
*Hanna is a freelance writer and a
journalist based in Nashville.*

We sort of suspected that we had done everything
that was required to make babies, but we weren't
sure. That's how naïve we were when I got pregnant; me at seventeen, Harry at nineteen, in a small
town in Tennessee.

Our marriage continued in that state of unen-
lightened grace until Harry's accidental death.
Missionary position, twice a week, with love and
sincerity for ten brief moments, concluding in one
orgasm—his.

A year after Harry's death, I began to feel
guilty because I started to think about sex—possibly
orgasmic sex—with another man. Or other men. I
had been reading Nancy Friday, Gael Greene, and
Anaïs Nin—and while I had sexual theory down pat
at thirty, I had zero hands on experience.

It was in this state of horny innocence that I
spied an attractive twenty-six year old man in my
Church of Christ Sunday School class. He had a
gorgeous body, the long fingers of an artist, and a

gift for words. Although he had a Ph.D. in philosophy, he was a cabinetmaker by trade.

Some people are visual, some people are feeling, some people, like me, respond to sound. He had a wonderful voice, like sterling silver against midnight blue velvet. When he objected to Sunday School dogma with quotations from Kierkegaard, he slew me.

At the appropriate moment, I complimented his comments, noting that at Church of Christ college they didn't teach me anything that might turn me away from the Bible. "Well, would you like to talk about these things?" the philosopher asked.

That's the way it started. He would call me at 10 P.M. and we'd talk until three in the morning, three nights a week. Several weeks into the conversations, the tone turned sexual. So when the master of Kierkegaard said, "I think we need to get together some afternoon," I pretty much knew what was going to happen.

The afternoon began with a pornographic movie. I had never seen an X-rated film. Within twenty minutes, it worked.

Panting as he yanked off my clothes, we tumbled into bed in his white on white bedroom. We wrestled around for a few minutes, and then suddenly he jumped up and began to rummage through his closet. Within seconds he pulled out four, patterned, silk neckties and asked with a sardonic grin, "Would you like to be tied up?"

"I wouldn't," I responded very matter-of-factly, "but thank you very much for asking." He shrugged, tossed the ties back into the closet, and resumed his attack with all the warmth of a death row aerobics instructor.

The only position I was not in that day was hanging from the rafters by my heels. We were backwards, forwards, hanging off the bed, hanging from the window ledge, reaching up from the floor, with him constantly checking with me on the quality of his performance. I was sore for three days just from the contortions. The jaded philosopher claimed he needed the variety because he'd been with three hundred women so now it took a little more excitement for him to maintain a continuous erection.

Finally, after ninety minutes of this exhausting, flawless—but cold—demonstration of his abilities, he climaxed (alone), rolled over, and announced that he had to go pay his phone bill before the office closed. "Could you leave now?" He didn't need to explain anything else. Embarrassed and annoyed, I threw on my clothes and drove home, relieved to know that I would never hear from this cruel man again.

When he called two weeks later to inform me that he had contracted an unspecified venereal disease from me, I was doubly surprised. I assured him that I couldn't have given it to him since I hadn't been with anybody except him in months.

The philosopher insisted I was wrong. Adamant to prove my position, I went to the doctor, came up clean and reported my results. Then I never did hear from him again.

I did, however, hear from his fiancée of two years, the one he failed to mention. She informed me with great glee that the philosopher called all of his one-night stands two weeks after the encounter because he had herpes and wanted a doctor to give his dates the bad news just as the virus was about to break out. She had contracted the disease from him, as had many others, but she thought his infidelities had ceased until she heard about our little roll in the hay from a mutual friend.

I thanked her for the information about our shared mate, expressed my condolences, apologized for my innocence and asked for her forgiveness. Then I quit Sunday School and the church, and never accepted a one-night stand again.

Daffy Dan

NORMA WEAVER

*Born in Massachusetts, Norma has
worked as an executive secretary for a
variety of firms on the East Coast.
She now lives in South Carolina.*

When a good-looking twenty-year-old boy I'd dated a few times in high school asked if I'd like to see the Red Sox play the Yankees, I accepted right away. That was a big game in Massachusetts because the Red Sox and Yankees had been fierce rivals for many years. I figured that since our previous dates had been enjoyable, we'd surely have a fun day.

My date didn't own a car, so he said we'd take the bus to Boston. Back in 1950, it was a two-hour, bumpy ride. There was no interstate between our hometown and the city.

On the Saturday of the game, I met him at the bus station. He purchased the tickets and then suggested, "Let's get something to read on the way." I was one of those Saturday afternoon movie kids when I was growing up so I selected my favorite movie magazine. He chose one from a Walt Disney comic book series, generally preferred by nine- and ten-year-olds. I said, "Oh you're kidding. Are you really buying that?"

"What's the matter? I love this comic book," he replied innocently.

He bought the books and we climbed onto the bus. I wanted to sit in one of those two seaters on the side. He insisted we take over the long bench seat in the back (probably because of his long legs).

Once the bus rolled, I began reading my movie book and he began reading his funny book. All of a sudden, he started screeching and howling. People turned around and stared. I looked at him wondering why he was making such a fuss in front of all those passengers. He just hooted again and turned the page of his book.

"Oh, Huey, Duey, and Louie, I love them!" he exclaimed like a gleeful nine-year-old. I could feel my face flush. I crunched down in the back seat and hid my face behind my movie magazine. When I peeked out I noticed people weren't giving him dirty looks, but they were fairly incredulous.

"Oh God," he laughed, "that Pluto is so funny," as if he was talking about a real dog. By now he was entertaining everybody on the bus. People were smirking and snickering, nudging each other, and giggling. One old gentleman who knew I was embarrassed winked at me like he was getting a kick out of it.

This went on and on. Finally I reached my boiling point. He was bent over cackling when he leaned over and started poking me in the elbow. "What?" I said with annoyance.

He pushed the book in my hands. "You have to read Goofy. You have to read Goofy." He was in hysterics.

I just stared at him and said coldly, "I don't have to read Goofy. I'm with Goofy." He just laughed even more.

Thankfully when we got to Boston, he left his comic book on the seat, and went back to being a normal person. Then things improved. We not only had a nice time at the ballgame, we were also fortunate enough to see the Red Sox beat the Yankees, which didn't happen too often back then.

Animal Attraction

BRIAN SOKOLOW
*By day, Brian is a retail merchandising
consultant in Baltimore. By night, he
works as a nightclub disc jockey,
specializing in divorce parties.*

She had a really trashy house. She herself wasn't so trashy. Blonde, blue-eyed, tall, pretty, big-breasted. Just my type. Any guy's type, a walking dream, a shiksa goddess.

She wasn't apologetic about the piles of clothing and dishes, newspapers and towels, half-full drink glasses, and month-old gum wrappers. To her, this state was normal. Otherwise she was too.

Since I didn't know Washington, D.C. well, we decided she should drive. Her car looked like her house on wheels with one exception. It was equally weathered on the outside and the inside because the windows had been permanently fixed in the down position for at least two years.

I parted some sun-bleached newspapers and sat down in the front. Instantly, a yellow jacket that had come up for air from eating a chunk of dried out pizza stung me in the ankle. There seemed to be a hive in the car. I mentioned the sting to her with a quick "Ow." She merely shrugged. The attack was as commonplace to her as the mess in her house. It wasn't to me. By midnight, my ankle was as big as a bowling ball.

My date slung a large bag over her shoulder and led me into the Mediterranean restaurant she had chosen. The bag was one of those funky looking, woven wood and yarn things, the kind everyone carried around in 1969, along with their floppy hats and pounds of make-up. Of course I didn't ask why a twenty-four-year-old woman was toting such a handbag around in the late '80s. I was a gentleman.

As we opened our menus, she announced with a giggle that she had to have grapes for dinner. "Fine," I said, "this is a Mediterranean restaurant, why don't you order grape leaves? I'll have the chicken with grapes."

When the meal arrived, she took a couple of bites, then grabbed the grapes off of both of our plates and dropped them into her bag. I asked her why. She pointed, "Look in the bag." Inside was this creature—one of those Indonesian-Malaysian monkeys, the kind you see swinging from vines on a National Geographic special—shoving a grape into its mouth! Was this thing responsible for the mess in her house?

"Don't you like animals?" she inquired with a pout as I stared at the poor monkey, wondering why she carried him around in a bag made to hold crocheting equipment, not wild animals.

"I think animals are great," I muttered awkwardly. "One time I had nine cats all at once. Of course, none of them were mine. They belonged to my roommate. I grew up with dogs, cats, iguanas, Gila monsters, and snakes. I get on famously with most animals." Even small monkeys named Junior.

Next stop on the date was the movies. *Fatal Attraction* was at the height of its popularity and the theater was packed. Not surprisingly, she refused to leave "that thing" in the car. "I take Junior to shopping malls and everywhere," she insisted coyly. "Besides, I can't roll up the windows, so he might get loose."

"And we wouldn't want Junior to get stung by a bee."

"No we wouldn't."

She tucked her bag under the seat before the movie started. Periodically, she checked to make sure Junior was okay. Everything was fine until Glenn Close, the crazy woman in the movie, booby-trapped the couple's summer home and Anne Archer was just about to discover their pet rabbit was in a pot boiling on the stove. It was at this climactic moment that my date discovered her monkey had escaped. Art imitating life or vice versa. In retrospect the juxtaposition is hilarious, but at the time nothing was funny.

She hunted around in the dark, but couldn't find him. I located the manager and told him what had happened. His face went ashen. It was only his

183

second week in his position and he wasn't sure what to do. Panicked, he locked the doors, turned up the house lights, stopped the movie, and announced that there was a problem. However, he didn't reveal what that problem was. Most people assumed it was some kind of technical difficulty instead of a wild animal running loose among the spilled diet cokes.

As the five hundred disgruntled people filed out, the three of us began a row by row search. We finally found the beast sitting in a popcorn tub, gorging himself.

My date scooped up her pet and headed for the door. To her surprise, the police stopped her. "Where's the license for this creature?" they demanded in their best Washington D.C.-drug-and-murder-capital-of-the-world tone.

"What license? How dare you barge in here like this?" she shouted back in outrage. She just couldn't understand what the big deal was. For an instant I thought the police might think we were refreshing diversion from the drug trade. They didn't see it that way. We were just another set of offenders who created a public nuisance on a Saturday night and deserved a verbal beating.

The more she yelled, the more the police yelled, and the more my ankle swelled. It was right out of a Peter Sellers movie. Finally, the police gave up in disgust and sent us home without a citation.

About midnight we arrived back at her house. I jumped out of the car, thanked her for an "interesting evening," and made a beeline to the emergency room for a large shot of antihistamine.

Trick or Treat

NORMA LENHART

*Born in Akron, Norma attended
business college then moved to
New York. She worked for the*
Journal American *newspaper and
an aircraft plant. She now lives
in Ohio and writes poetry.*

When I was nineteen years old, I used to go down to dances at the YWCA in Akron, Ohio. This one particular night I went by myself because my girlfriend couldn't go along, and I met this very wholesome looking, handsome, polite, young man. He was my idea of a prince charming. We did a lot of laughing and a lot of talking, as well as a lot of dancing. In fact, I didn't dance with anyone else that evening after I met him.

Towards the end of the dance, he offered to take me home. I declined. However, I did give him my telephone number. The following night he called to ask if I wanted to accompany him to a Halloween party at his friend's house the next weekend.

A couple of hours before we were to go out to the masquerade, I heard a knock on my door. I went to see who was there. A tiny voice said, "It's me." I figured it was one of the kids in the neighborhood trick-or-treating.

I opened the door and oh, boy, there he was. His costume consisted of a moustache, a long, gray coat, shoes with no socks, and a big smile. "Hi," I said. He stood there for a second grinning. Then he threw open his coat and cried, "Trick or treat!" Under the coat, he was naked as a jaybird.

I slammed the door shut. He pounded on the door, "Open up. Open up. Aren't you gonna go? Aren't you gonna go?" Frightened, embarrassed, and shaking, I grabbed the nearest phone and called the police. He obviously heard me because right away I heard his car door slam and his vehicle pull out.

The police came. That was fine. But on their way out they snickered. So did my girlfriend when I called her to tell her my story. "It wouldn't be so funny if it happened to you," I insisted, trying to cover my doubly hurt feelings.

She continued to laugh, "Well, I thought everybody knew he was a weirdo."

That weirdo kept me away from those dances for almost two years. However, when I finally did find the courage to return, I met my husband of the last forty-seven years.

$\mathcal{L}$ove $\mathcal{S}$tinks

JEAN DEAN
*Jean was a model in Texas at the
time of her date. Now a grandmother,
she lives in Northern California,
where she does charity work for
the Peninsula Humane Society.*

My friends had asked me to organize a party out
on Galveston Beach and I had everything in order.
But on the drive south from Houston, I suddenly
realized that I had forgotten the firewood. I didn't
know what I was going to do until my date pulled
into a convenience store to buy some ice and I saw
a huge pile of logs sitting out back. What a great
bonfire it would make. So, while my date shopped,
I lugged the long boards over to his brand new
Oldsmobile, maneuvered them into the back seat,
and opened up the back window to let the longest
planks stick out.

About five minutes out of the parking lot, I
noticed a noxious odor polluting the car. I glanced
at my date, assuming he had severe indigestion. He
didn't say anything. I didn't feel comfortable asking because, well, it was only our third date.

As the minutes passed, the odor grew worse and worse. I looked at him again, wondering what was going on. He looked at me, wondering as well. I said nothing. He said nothing. We were both too polite. So he turned on the air conditioning and drove on in silence. Finally, he just couldn't stand it any longer and said, "What is that odor?"

"I don't know."

We pulled over to the side of the road, turned on the lights and there it was: I had lime residue all over my brand new black pants and black knit leopard top. There was lime residue all over the brand new Oldsmobile, and lime residue on the logs. Smelly lime! In the dark, I obviously didn't realize that what I thought was great firewood, was in fact the remains of an old outhouse in which they clearly used lime as a deodorizer. We just couldn't believe it.

In Texas in 1957, there were a lot of open fields. At the first one we saw, we got rid of the logs. Then we pulled into the nearest service station and I tried to use some paper towels to wipe off my clothes. It was futile. The outfit was totally ruined. But because we were hours from home and our friends were all waiting for us on the beach, we just kept on driving.

Our friends at the party laughed when we told them the story and understandably kept their distance. We didn't keep our distance from each other, however, and within ten months we were married.

It was just one of the funny things that happened to us, that made us know we were meant for
each other.

Sorority Sisters

PETER NICHOLS

*Peter is an entertainment lawyer
practicing in Los Angeles. Now happily
married, he has not yet confused his
two-year-old daughter with anyone
else in her playgroup.*

It was the dead of winter, I was a sophomore in college, and I was acting in a play called *Love's Labour's Lost*. We were about to have a weekend night off, and someone in the cast said that I should go out with a woman named Diane. He said she was a great girl. That I would like her. That she had a great sense of humor. Nevertheless, I was a bit dubious. Diane was a sorority girl, and I was not big on sororities or fraternities.

I call her up, "Fine. Friday night. I'll pick you up—"

I didn't have a car at the time, so I had to borrow a car from a friend. A Corvair convertible. It was not the best car, but he was the best friend I had who had a car.

It's Chicago. It's early February. I go get the car, have trouble starting it. I'm a little bit nervous and a little late and now it starts to rain. I pull up to the sorority, and between parking the car and running to the front door, I get totally soaked. I stand out there, trying to absorb a little more water, waiting for someone to come and let me in. Finally a young woman opens the door.

"Peter?"

"Yes. Diane?"

"Yes."

We drive to downtown Chicago. Because it's raining, we have the windows rolled all the way up, and because it's an old car, all the exhaust is coming in. We're choking. Our eyes are tearing. We're getting headaches. It's terrible.

We have absolutely nothing to say to each other. She's a math major from a small town in Iowa. She wants to become an accountant and go back to the farm, get married, and breed children. I'm a theater major from the Lower East Side of Manhattan. I want to produce and direct modern versions of Shakespearean plays for television. I have a joint with me and offer to share it with her. She's never smoked anything and immediately thinks I am a charter member of the Manson family.

We go to this play on the South Side of Chicago. It's an Off-Broadway kind of play that's supposed to be a drawing room comedy, but nothing's funny. I'm bored. I hate it. She's bored. She hates it. But we're both too polite to just admit it and leave.

By the time we get out of the play, the temperature has dropped to five degrees below zero, as it can in Chicago, and all of the roads are glazed ice. The Corvair has bald tires. I'm spinning and skidding. It's snowing now. She's almost in tears, the poor woman.

We stop at this jazz club—the Blue Note, the Blue Willow, the Blue Tree, something like that—and listen to some jazz. She doesn't like jazz. I love jazz. The food arrives. The waiter spills soup on her lap. By now, she's at the edge of hysteria.

We leave. She's got a big patch of soup on her dress. I'm really embarrassed. I haven't had anything to say to her all night. We get into the car. It won't start.

It's snowing. Glazed ice. We're in the middle of the South Side of Chicago. The campus is on the North Side. I don't have credit cards. I don't have Triple A. She didn't even bring her wallet. We're stranded.

I ditch the car and we take a cab all the way back to my dorm. I leave her, waiting outside in the cab, while I go inside and wake up five of my friends in order to raise the money to pay the fare.

I shake her hand as I drop her off at her sorority, go back home and call the friend who set me up with this woman.

"It was terrible! We had nothing to say to each other. We were totally different!"

193

"That's incredible," my friend says, "I just got a call from Diane saying that she had a great time."

I couldn't believe it. "You got a call from Diane Jason saying she had a great time?"

"Diane Jason? Who the hell is Diane Jason?"

It seems there was another girl named Diane, who was supposed to be set up with me, and this Diane Jason person was supposed to be set up with another guy named Peter, who, it seems, showed at the sorority fifteen minutes later. In other words, we'd gone out with the wrong people. But it wasn't the wrong people for those two, because that Diane and that Peter got married soon after graduation.

The Great Outdoors

JANE ABBOTT

*Jane is a marketing consultant in
the entertainment field.*

It was hard to take Michael seriously. He was barely twenty to my worldly twenty-six, sweet, funny, and cute too. Yet, he kept hanging around. And when he asked me to marry him in front of about a hundred people in a crowded restaurant where we both worked, I didn't have the heart to say no.

About a month before the wedding, my brother Rich came to visit us. It was August in sweltering Arizona, and the only tolerable outdoor pastime was tubing down the Salt River. Michael had this great idea. He would arrange this tubing expedition for the three of us. I was just supposed to relax and enjoy it.

The first clue that this laissez-faire attitude was a tad optimistic came when we got to the river that morning and unloaded the tubes. Michael had bought these little black rubber donuts—not the giant truck tries you're supposed to use for this abusive activity. "Did you check for leaks?" I inquired, staying calm.

"You're worried about nothing," Michael bragged as he lashed our cooler to the fourth inner tube and placed this little Tupperware container on top of it.

"A deal's a deal," I told myself grimly, and mounted my tube in the ice water.

The tubes were so small we perched on top of them instead of sitting in them, which gave onlookers the curious impression that we were sliding along on top of the water. And sure enough, before we passed the first grove of cottonwoods, our "rafts" began to lose air. We were sinking into the freezing, churning water.

"What's in that little plastic container?" I hollered over the roar of the first set of rapids. "Shouldn't that be inside the cooler?"

"Don't worry about it," Mr. Sportsman retorted. We hit the rapids, and as expected, that Tupperware container took a flying leap into the air and disappeared into the water. Michael blanched.

"What was in that?"

"Oh nothing, just my car keys."

"Your *car keys*? You mean we're stranded?"

Turns out not only the car keys were lost, but also the little bit of money Michael had brought along. We searched furtively along the bottom of the river. Nothing turned up. My brother, "Mr. What, Me Worry?", waited patiently while I fumed and Michael tried to save face. Finally, I noticed that we had wandered far from the "civilized" side of the river and were almost to the opposite bank. It was too dangerous to swim across. All the stories I'd ever heard about people being sucked under by pockets of wild water and discovered days later, trapped in underwater tree branches, came flooding into my head.

"We'll just walk across to the other side," announced Michael, still Mr. Know-It-All.

"Like hell we will," I snapped back, looking from the whitecaps to our pitiful, flabby inner tubes. This had gone on long enough—I was taking charge. "We'll walk along this bank—on dry land—until the water is calmer and we can get across safely."

Rich was not about to be deterred by these petty domestic quarrels. He climbed back on his black, rubber pancake and sailed off. Then Michael and I began our trudge along the riverbank, looking for a place to ford.

On and on we walked, scorched by the midday heat. Instead of narrowing, the river got wider and wilder until we could barely see the opposite shore. Our side of the riverbank grew rougher and steeper. By now we were 100 feet above the treacherous flow and still climbing.

No longer concerned about drowning, I was now terrified we might die of exposure here in the wilds of the Arizona desert. Michael had no more suggestions—I had verbally whipped him into silence. An overhead buzzing sound interrupted our standoff. From over the hill, a helicopter appeared, flying so low it nearly grazed our heads. An unintelligible voice blared from a megaphone.

War maneuvers! I knew that the military sometimes used this area as a training ground. We tried to make ourselves inconspicuous while at the same time identifying ourselves as friendly—if stupid—trespassers. The helicopter circled several times and disappeared. Crestfallen, we plodded onward.

Soon, a Bronco-like vehicle piloted by a little guy in khaki shorts rolled over the top of a hill. "Are you hurt?" the energetic forest ranger yelled.

"No, just lost," we answered. He seemed disappointed. In hostile silence, Michael and I climbed aboard.

For the next half hour, we wound our way around this mountain, driving along paths barely wide enough for a mountain goat. When we finally reached the tubers' rendezvous point, it was impossible to tell where Michael's flush of embarrassment ended and his sunburn began. I was fit to be tied. The one relief was the sight of my brother Rich calmly lounging in the shade.

That left the slight problem of getting home. Michael's spare change was at the bottom of the river, Rich never had any money in his pocket or his bathing suit, and my cash was safely stowed away—under the seat of the locked car. I made the boys panhandle twenty cents to call one of my bridesmaids. She was willing to make a three-hour round trip out to rescue us—not just to pick us up, but to call a locksmith, make arrangements for him to meet us at the car, and loan us money to pay him. All in 120-degree heat. Now that's friendship.

By the time our savior got there, I had figured out fifty ways to call off a wedding. My friend, a born-again Christian, lectured me about forgiveness on the tense ride home. Unfortunately her words fell on deaf ears that day.

Or maybe not. That was nineteen years ago. Since then, Michael has grown up and I've lightened up. We've been happily married most of the time we've been together and we now have a son. We've taken a lot of fun trips, but we've never again tackled the great outdoors.

About the Author

Carole Markin is an author, screenwriter, independent filmmaker, and artist. A graduate of Harvard Radcliffe College and the Directing Fellowship at the American Film Institute, she has been an executive in public television and served as President of Independent Feature Project/West, an organization of 3,000 independent filmmakers. Since the publication of her first book, *Bad Dates*, she has become an unofficial dating expert. She resides in Los Angeles, California.